Excel for Windows

A Visual Approach for the Beginner

Welcome to **Quick & Easy.** Designed for the true novice, this new series covers basic tasks in a simple, learn-by-doing fashion. If that sounds like old news to you, take a closer look.

Quick & Easy books are a bit like picture books. They're for people who would rather see and do than read and ponder. The books are colorful. They're full of illustrations and accompanying text that is straightforward, concise, and easy to read.

But don't waste your time reading about our **Quick & Easy** books; start learning your new software package instead. This **Quick & Easy** book is just the place to start.

Excel for Windows™
Quick & Easy

Gerald E. Jones

SYBEX®

San Francisco • Paris • Düsseldorf • Soest

Acquisitions Editor: David J. Clark
Series Editor: Christian T. S. Crumlish
Editor: Richard Mills
Technical Editor: Ellen Ferlazzo
Word Processor: Ann Dunn
Book Designer: Helen Bruno
Typesetters: Claudia Smelser, Dina F Quan
Proofreader/Production Assistant: David Silva
Indexer: Ted Laux
Cover Designer: Archer Design
Cover Illustrator: Richard Miller

Library of Congress Card Number: 92-82552
ISBN: 0-7821-1121-1

Manufactured in the United States of America
10 9 8 7 6 5 4 3 2 1

ACKNOWLEDGMENTS

A team of dedicated professionals worked to develop and produce this book. At SYBEX, thanks to Dave Clark, acquisitions editor; Christian Crumlish, series editor; Richard Mills, editor; and Ellen Ferlazzo, technical editor. Special thanks to Peter Nathan, Senior Decision Support Analyst at Paramount Pictures, for suggesting the design of the check register example. And personal thanks, as always, to Georja Jones, who is just dynamic.

Contents
at a Glance

●

Contents

INTRODUCTION

●

This book is intended to help you *learn by doing*. Specifically, its subject is Microsoft Excel 4.0 for Windows. But the broader aim of the book is to help you solve practical problems. The focus is on problems in business, the kinds of tasks and assignments that you encounter every day. For example, almost everyone has to balance a checkbook or turn in an employee expense report, so these are precisely the tasks that are used as examples in this book. You will create an electronic check register that can generate an ongoing balance, and you will design and print an expense report. These will be fully workable, practical tools that you can use long after you no longer need them as learning aids.

How to Use This Book

You need little or no prior knowledge of either Windows or Excel to use this book successfully.

In approach, *Excel for Windows Quick & Easy* is a book to be used rather than simply read. It should be on your desk to guide you as you sit at your computer and work through its exercises. Each lesson is a short work session that can be performed in about ten minutes. Each one focuses on a set of program features that can be applied to a practical problem—such as balancing a checkbook. Lessons are organized to be done in sequence, though not necessarily all at once—one or two lessons per day is a good pace. If several days pass between lessons, glance back at the previous lesson as a quick review before you continue. The sequence naturally begins with very basic operations and tasks, and makes a logical, step-by-step progression toward more ambitious assignments.

Always try to work through a lesson in its entirety. The procedures prompt you to save your work to disk at the end of each lesson. If, for some reason, you must stop work in the middle of a lesson, *be sure to save your work!* Remember that electronic computer memory is not permanent. If you do not save your work to a disk file, it will be lost when power to the computer is turned off.

There are two fundamental elements to the presentation: *procedural steps* and *visual references*. The procedural steps are numbered computer operations. You will read each step and then perform it using the mouse or keyboard as you work with Excel. After every few steps, a color picture of the computer screen is shown. This is your visual reference—a snapshot, in effect, of what your screen should look like as you are executing a procedure. With this unique visual approach, you won't go astray. (Or, if you do, you won't go very far astray!)

Here is an example of a numbered step accompanied by a screen display:

2. Click the **AutoSum** tool in the toolbar near the top center of the screen.

AutoSum tool

Occasionally, the text will be supplemented with a Note, which may highlight an alternate method, provide a reminder, or alert you to possible difficulties.

Most of the procedures assume that you will be using the mouse to make selections. Keyboard selections usually are described only when pressing a key is the quickest or most natural way to do something.

This book truly aims to deliver on the promise of its title—namely, that learning Excel can be *quick* and *easy.* You are not necessarily learning Excel because you enjoy investigating new computer software products. You want the minimum, essential information for getting the job done. Consequently, each session concludes with some functional result, which you will save immediately to disk for your ongoing use. Since each lesson requires only minutes to complete, you can work through the steps whenever you have just a little time—on a coffee break, between phone calls, or perhaps just to get a quick sense of accomplishment before ending your workday.

Using Windows

Here's a brief summary of basic Windows operations. For more information, see the *Microsoft Windows User's Guide.*

Making Selections with a Mouse

A mouse is a movable device for pointing and making selections on the computer screen. As you move the mouse around on your desktop, a small symbol called a *pointer* moves along with it on the screen. The pointer can change shape to indicate the type of selection being made.

There are three main types of actions that can be performed by pressing the left mouse button:

> **Clicking:** Point to the item you want and press the left button once, briefly.

Double clicking: Point to the item and click the left button twice rapidly.

Dragging: Point to an item, press and hold down the left button, continue to hold down the button as you move the mouse to a new location, and then release the button.

Menu Selections

Options you can select in Windows and Excel appear in a *menu bar* beneath the *title bar* of the program window. A window represents a currently running task or open document. The title bar gives the name of the window. The title bar and start-up menu bar of Excel appear at the top of the screen:

To make a selection from a menu bar, follow these steps:

1. Click the menu item you want, such as **File,** or press **Alt,** then the underscored letter of the item you want.

2. Select a command from the pull-down menu that appears. Click the item with the mouse, or press its underscored letter on the keyboard.

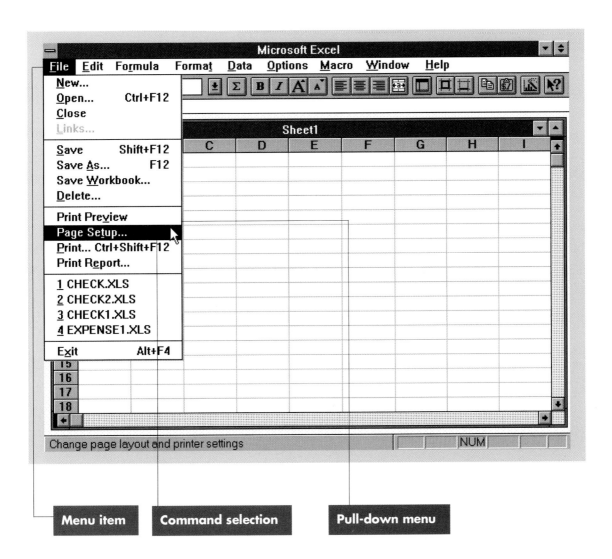

Menu item   **Command selection**   **Pull-down menu**

Getting Help

To display a window containing explanatory text on any action within
Windows or Excel, press F1. You can get a listing of Help topics (or search
for specific topics by name) by selecting Help from the menu bar.

Don't let the technicalities here discourage you. You don't need any special knowledge before you start work. If you know how to point and click with the mouse, you have ample preparation. If you can devote a few minutes to working through Lesson 1, you will see for yourself how learning Excel for Windows can be quick and easy!

Getting Acquainted with Worksheets

In this lesson, you will learn about the basic elements of an electronic document called a *worksheet*. A worksheet is simply an accounting-style spreadsheet that can be held in computer memory and stored on disk. In following the steps below, you will build a type of worksheet you probably use every day—a check register.

This book is all about learning by doing, so turn on your computer and get started.

● Note The discussion assumes that you are already familiar with Windows controls. Specifically, you need to know how to use the mouse or keyboard to make selections, including executing commands from pull-down menus. In this book, procedures that involve a sequence of menu selections are shown with the commands linked by the ➤ symbol. For example, when the procedure directs you to select File ➤ Open, you pull down the File menu and select the Open command. You'll find a brief summary of basic operations and commands for Windows in the Introduction.

Starting Windows and Excel

Your system may be set up to start Windows automatically. If not, the DOS prompt will appear at the top left of the screen:

    C:>

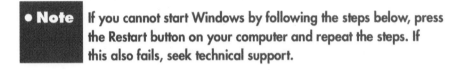

A different letter (disk drive) or group of letters (path) may appear, especially if you are connected to a network. If you have a hard disk, you will probably see the C:> prompt.

> **● Note** If you cannot start Windows by following the steps below, press the Restart button on your computer and repeat the steps. If this also fails, seek technical support.

1. Type **win**, then press ↵. Microsoft Windows will start, and its Program Manager window will open.

2. Open the program group labeled **Microsoft Excel 4.0**. (Point to its icon with the mouse and double-click with the left button. Or, move the highlight to it with the cursor keys and then select **File ➤ Open** by pulling down the **File** menu and selecting the **Open** command.)

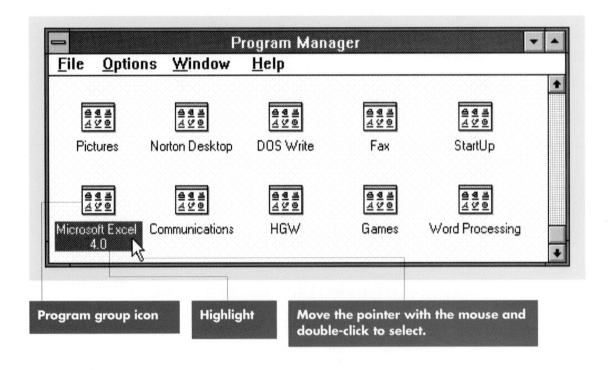

3. The Excel application window will open. Select the program icon Microsoft Excel.

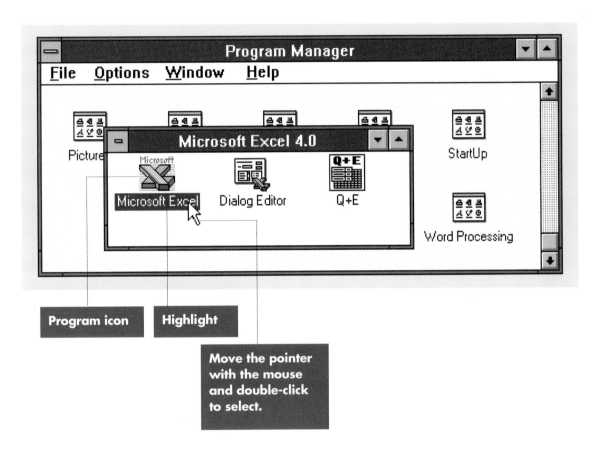

Program icon

Highlight

Move the pointer with the mouse and double-click to select.

The program will start, and a blank worksheet will appear. The worksheet is contained in a *document window,* and its temporary title is Sheet1. You will be building your check register in this worksheet.

Quick&Easy

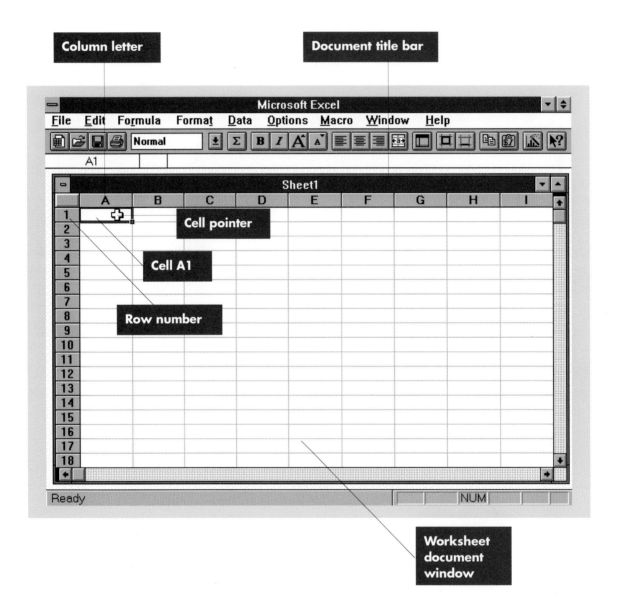

Column letter

Document title bar

Cell pointer

Cell A1

Row number

Worksheet
document
window

Exploring The Worksheet

Notice that the worksheet, or *sheet,* is composed of small rectangular
areas, or *cells.* The cells are arranged in columns and rows. In the visible portion of the sheet, the columns are labeled from left to right with

the letters A–I. The rows are numbered from top to bottom 1–18. (The sheet can actually be much larger than this, but this area is a comfortable size for now.)

Any cell in the sheet can be identified by the letter of its column and the number of its row, such as A1. This identifier is called a *cell reference,* or *cell address.*

The current cell, or *active cell,* is surrounded by a highlight. When just one cell is active, the highlight is an outline.

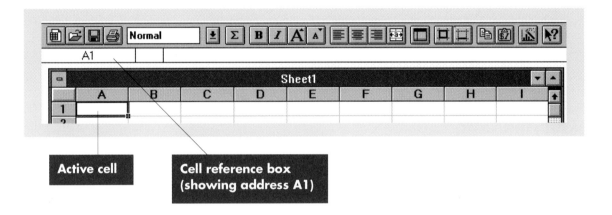

Active cell

Cell reference box (showing address A1)

When the program starts and opens Sheet1, the cell in the top-left corner of the sheet is highlighted. This is cell A1.

Selecting a Cell

In Excel, you must select a cell before you can enter data into it. Here's how the selection works.

- Click a different cell within the sheet—**C4**—the cell in column C, row 4. The highlight will move as you move the cell pointer (a hollow plus sign) with the mouse. Note that the address (C4) of the selected, or active, cell appears in the *active cell reference* box just above the sheet window at the top left of the screen.

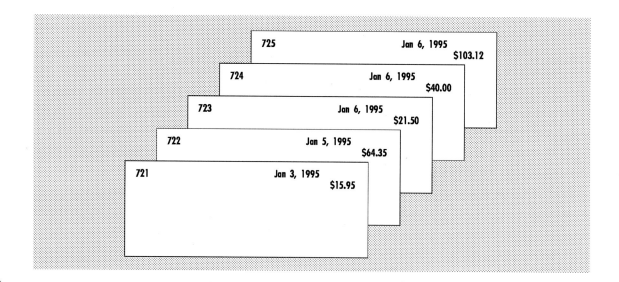

Cell pointer   Cell C4   Cell highlight

Entering Data

The example in this lesson will be a check register, a record of debits and credits to a checking account. Assume that you have a stack of checks. You can begin to build the register by entering their amounts into the sheet.

1. With the highlight still in cell C4, type the amount of the first check: **15.95**. (Make sure Num Lock is on if you are using the number keys on the separate keypad.)

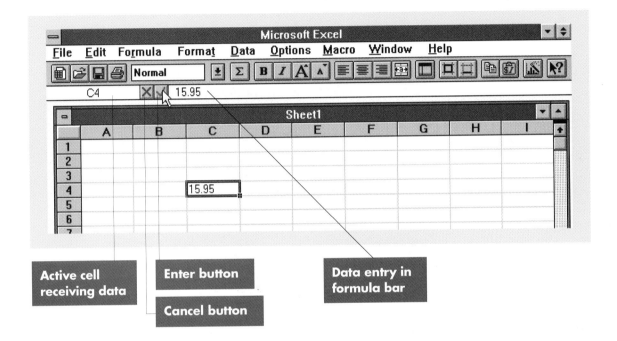

Active cell receiving data

Enter button

Cancel button

Data entry in formula bar

These digits, or numeric data, appear above the sheet in the *formula bar* as you press the character keys. Just to the left of this text box is a pair of buttons, × and ✓. The × button means "Cancel," the equivalent of pressing Esc on the keyboard. The ✓ button means "Enter," the equivalent of pressing ↵.

2. Click the ✓ button or press ↵. The value 15.95 appears in cell C4. Note that this numeric entry is right-aligned, or justified at the right edge of the cell.

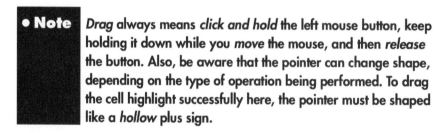

Entering Data in a Range of Cells

A block of cells is called a *range.* A column or a row is a type of range. A range can contain multiple columns and rows, as long as the cells are contiguous, or next to one another.

You can highlight a range by *dragging* the cell pointer from one corner of the range to the other. Usually, you will want to start at the top-left cell of the range and drag to the cell at the bottom right.

If you specify a range in the sheet by highlighting the range first, the data you enter will flow into it. For example, you can enter the rest of the check amounts in a column.

> **● Note** *Drag* always means *click and hold* the left mouse button, keep holding it down while you *move* the mouse, and then *release* the button. Also, be aware that the pointer can change shape, depending on the type of operation being performed. To drag the cell highlight successfully here, the pointer must be shaped like a *hollow* plus sign.

Highlight the rest of the column that will hold the check amounts.

1. Click and hold the mouse button on cell C5.

2. Keep holding the mouse button down as you move the mouse to cell C8.

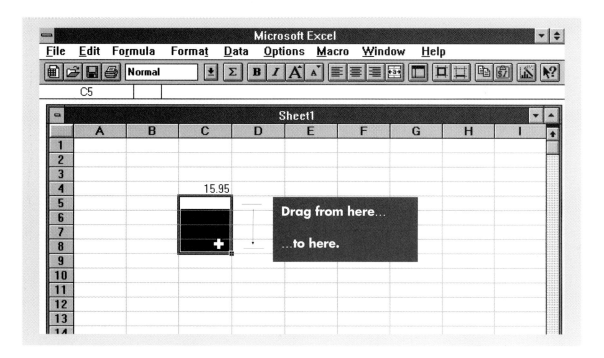

3. Release the mouse button.

4. Type the rest of the check amounts: **64.35, 21.50, 40.00,** and **103.12**. Press ↵ after each entry.

Note how the data flow into the area you highlighted in the sheet.

When you've made all the entries, the sheet should look like this:

Microsoft Excel									
File **Edit** **Formula** **Format** **Data** **Options** **Macro** **Window** **Help**									

Normal | Σ | B | I | A | A'

C5 | 64.35

Sheet1

	A	B	C	D	E	F	G	H	I
1									
2									
3									
4			15.95						
5			64.35						
6			21.5						
7			40						
8			103.12						
9									
10									
11									
12									
13									
14									

Summing the Items

It's time to get the program to do the work by generating a total of the check amounts you've entered.

1. Click the cell **C10**, which will hold the total.

2. Click the **AutoSum** tool in the toolbar near the top center of the screen.

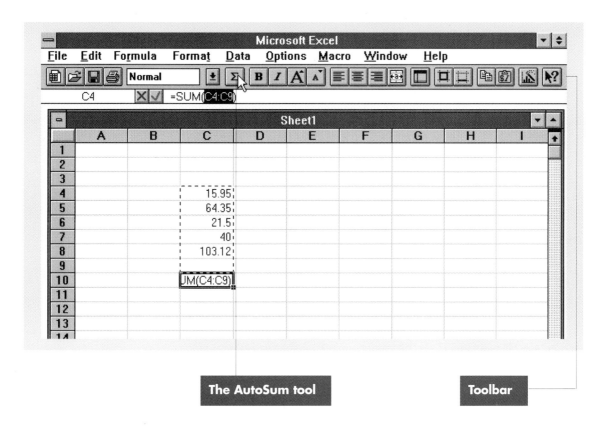

The AutoSum tool

Toolbar

3. In the formula bar, click the ✓ button to accept the entry.

The total will be inserted in the selected cell.

Your sheet should look like this:

	A	B	C	D	E	F	G	H	I
1									
2									
3									
4			15.95						
5			64.35						
6			21.5						
7			40						
8			103.12						
9									
10			244.92						
11									
12									

You've Reached a Milestone!

You've now reached an important milestone in your mastery of Excel for Windows. You have organized data as a range (a column, in this case) in a worksheet. You have also used a powerful feature of the program (AutoSum) to generate a useful result.

You may be pleasantly surprised to learn that many worksheet operations are no more complex than that!

Saving Your Work

You've expended some effort in generating this information. It is valuable, new work. You should store it so you can use it later.

When you are entering data into a worksheet, your entries are registered in the computer's random access memory (RAM). This is a kind of holding area for work-in-progress. However, when you turn off your computer, or even when it experiences a momentary loss of power for any reason, the contents of its memory will be lost. To save the information permanently, it is necessary to store it in a file on disk.

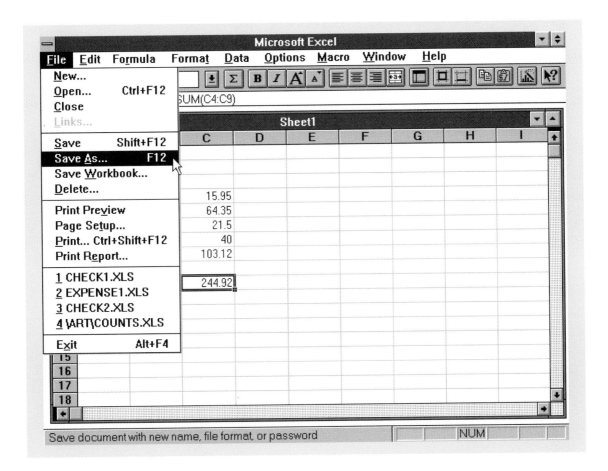

1. Select **File ➤ Save As.**

2. The Save As dialog box will appear. Notice that the program automatically assigns the name SHEET1.XLS. However, type the new name **check.xls**, and it will appear in the File Name text box. (The program will accept either uppercase or lowercase letters for file names.)

Quick Easy

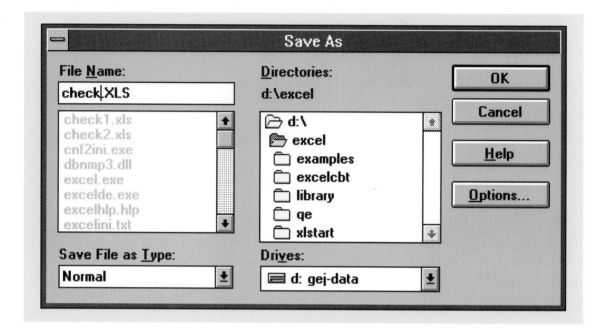

3. Select **OK**.

Your worksheet is now stored on disk, where it will remain even after your computer is turned off. In the next lesson, you will begin to concentrate more on the appearance of the worksheet.

Exiting the Program

If you do not plan to start Lesson 2 right away and want to quit working in Excel, follow this step:

● From the File menu, select Exit.

The Excel application window will close, and you will be returned to the Program Manager.

2 Laying Out a Worksheet

In this lesson, you will edit the worksheet CHECK.XLS that you created in Lesson 1. You will add descriptive labels to the sheet. You will also rearrange the display so that the numbers and letters of data values and labels align properly.

Reopening the Worksheet

To begin this session, reopen the worksheet by following these steps:

1. If you exited Excel at the end of the last lesson, restart the program by double-clicking its icon in the Windows Program Manager.

2. The start-up menu bar for Excel will appear. Select the **File** pull-down menu.

3. The program keeps track of the four files you worked on most recently. If you see CHECK.XLS listed at the bottom of the pull-down menu, click it to reopen the file. Or select **Open** and the Open dialog box will appear. Double-click the file name CHECK.XLS.

The worksheet will appear in an open document window in Excel. You are ready to resume work.

Quick&Easy

```
 ─                          Microsoft Excel                    ▼ ⬥
 File  Edit  Formula  Format  Data  Options  Macro  Window  Help
 [▨][▷][▨][🖨] │Normal      │ [±][Σ][B][I][A][Aˇ] [≡][≡][≡][⊞] [□][□][□] [▧][▨] [▨][▸?]
    A1            │          │
 ─                          CHECK.XLS                          ▼ ▲
        A       B       C       D       E       F       G       H       I      ▲
  1 ┌──────┐
  2 └──────┘
  3
  4                      15.95
  5                      64.35
  6                      21.5
  7                      40
  8                     103.12
  9
 10                     244.92
 11
 12
 13
 14
 15
 16
 17
 18                                                                           ▼
 ◄                                                                         ►
 Ready                                          │      │      │ NUM │
```

Formatting the Amounts as Currency

As you look again at the worksheet, do you notice that the program
truncated some of your entries? For example, 21.50 appears as 21.5,
and 40.00 appears as 40. That's because the program assumes a number
style of Normal, unless you specify something else. Normal style, or
number format, uses no commas as thousands separators (for example,
1000 instead of 1,000) and cuts off trailing zeros from decimal values.
This is not the way you are used to seeing monetary amounts, so it
will be necessary to change the display.

The format of a selected cell or range is shown in the Style drop-down
list box in the toolbar.

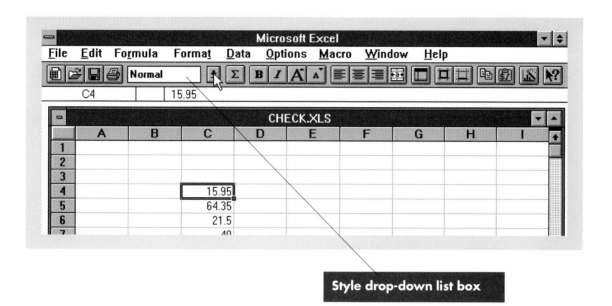

Style drop-down list box

Now change the number format of the range of check amounts and the total. You will select the Currency format, which includes a leading dollar sign and two decimal places for pennies.

1. Drag the cell pointer from cell **C4** to cell **C10**. This is the range C4:C10.

• Note The colon (:) here means "and all adjacent cells including." With this notation, you can specify a range by naming the cells at two of its corners.

2. Click on the **Style** box on the toolbar.

3. Select **Currency** from the drop-down list.

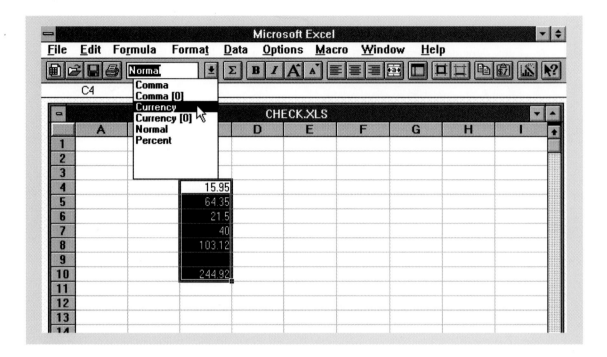

All of the entries in the range C4:C10 will be displayed in Currency format.

Labeling the Columns

If a worksheet were only a listing of check amounts, you could save yourself the trouble of learning how to use a spreadsheet and use a printing calculator instead. But an electronic worksheet is much more useful than that. Begin now to build something that looks a bit more like an actual check register—one that can balance itself! Start by labeling the columns.

1. Drag the pointer from **A2** to **E2** to highlight the row A2:E2.

2. Type labels as follows, pressing ↵ after each: **Date**, **Reference**, **Checks**, **Deposits**, and **Balance**. Notice how your entries flow into the selected range. When you are finished, your sheet should look like this:

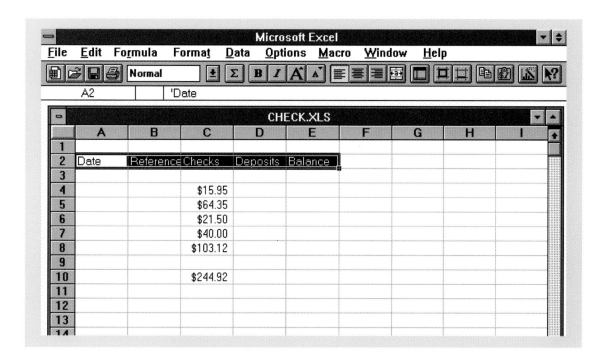

Centering the Labels over the Columns

The check register would be more attractive if the labels were centered over their respective columns. To do this, you should know about the ways in which labels can be aligned.

Notice that the text data appear in the formula bar preceded by an apostrophe, or single quotation mark ('):

'Date

The program inserts this character automatically when alphabetic characters are entered. It means "the left-aligned label," and indeed all the labels you entered are aligned, or justified, at the left edges of their cells.

 **● Note** If you do not see the prefix characters on your screen, Excel was probably installed without Lotus 1-2-3 help. If you want to see these characters, select Workspace from the Options menu and check Alternate Navigation Keys in the dialog box that appears.

Label formats can be controlled by the following leading characters, or prefixes:

'	Left alignment
^	Center alignment
"	Right alignment

However, you need not ever enter these prefixes. The program can do it for you, changing the alignment of an entire range in the process. Now, center the labels over the columns by following this step:

● While your entries in the row A2:E2 are still highlighted, click the Center Align tool in the toolbar. The labels will be moved to the centers of their cells, and the data prefixes will be changed to carets (^).

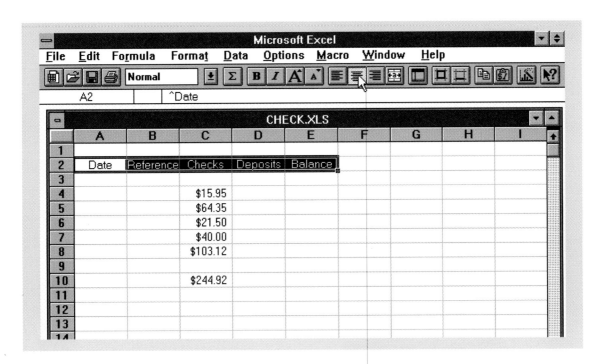

The Center Align tool

Applying Data Formats

The formatting of a cell or range can control the type of data entered into it, as well as the appearance of the data when displayed or printed out.

There are actually several ways to change the formatting of a selected cell or range. You've used the first way already—clicking the Style box in the toolbar. But the choices here are somewhat limited. In the following steps, you will use two different ways to change number formatting. Both work equally well. As you practice with Excel, you can use the method that seems most comfortable for you.

Changing the First Column to Date Format

The first column of the sheet you are building will hold dates of transactions. Since dates require a specific notation, it would be convenient to have Excel do the formatting automatically, just as it did for the currency amounts.

Remember that you must first highlight a cell or range before you can make menu selections, or use commands, that will affect it. To change the data format, follow these steps:

1. Drag the pointer from cell **A4** to cell **A9** to highlight the range A4:A9.

2. To see more choices for number formatting, select **Format** from the menu bar, then **Number**.

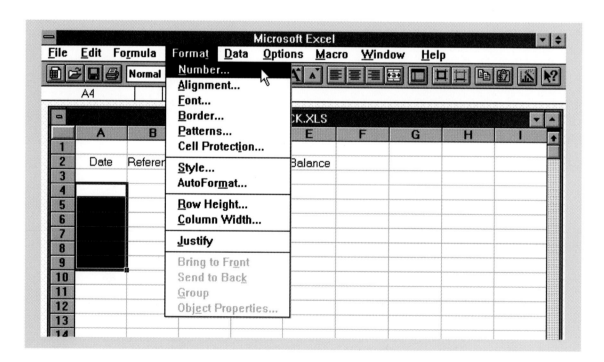

3. The Number Format dialog box will appear. Click **Date** (the type of format) in the Category list. (The top entry in the Format Codes list is already selected by default: **m/d/yy**.)

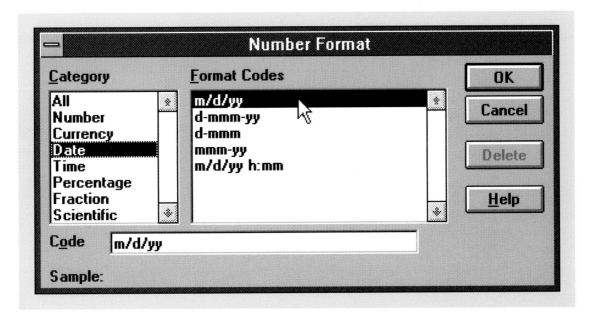

4. Select **OK** to close the dialog box.

Now, regardless of the way in which you enter dates into this column, the display will always have the form m/d/yy, where *m* is numeric month (1–12), *d* is day (1–31), and *yy* is the last two digits of the year. Enter the data now to see how this works.

5. With range A4:A9 still highlighted, type the following entries, pressing ↵ after each one:

1/3/95

1-5-1995

01-06-95

01/06/95

1/6/1995

Notice that, although you typed in dates in a variety of formats, the formatting you applied to the range generated a consistent format in the display.

	A	B	C	D	E	F	G	H	I
				CHECK.XLS					
1									
2	Date	Reference	Checks	Deposits	Balance				
3									
4	1/3/95		$15.95						
5	1/5/95		$64.35						
6	1/6/95		$21.50						
7	1/6/95		$40.00						
8	1/6/95		$103.12						
9									
10			$244.92						
11									
12									

Changing the Last Two Columns to Currency Format

The columns labeled Deposits and Balance will hold currency data and should be formatted accordingly. Although you could do this simply by making a selection from the Style drop-down list box (as you did previously), try another method. This is a shortcut that offers convenience as well as more choices.

1. Drag the pointer from cell **D4** to cell **E10** to highlight the range D4:E10.

2. Be sure that the pointer is within the selected range, and click the *right* mouse button. A shortcut menu will pop up.

3. From the shortcut menu, select **Number**.

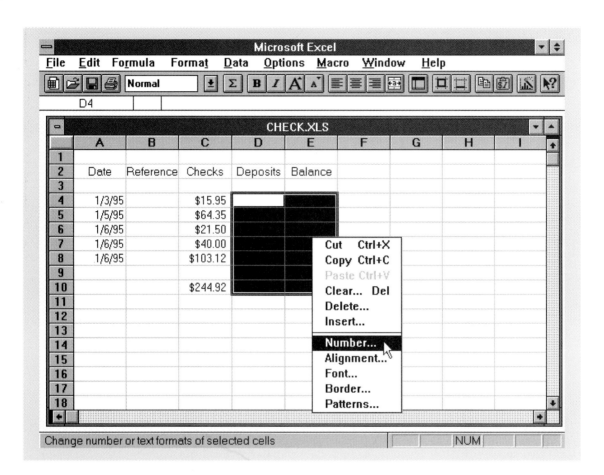

The Number Format dialog box will appear.

4. Select **Currency** from the Category list. Then select the third entry from the top in the Format Codes list: **$#,##0.00** (Currency format with two decimal places and a thousands separator).

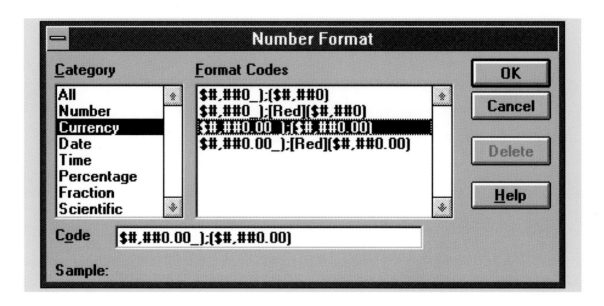

5. Select **OK** to close the dialog box.

Notice that this method of formatting is the same as selecting Format ➤ Number, since the same dialog box appears. However, using
the right mouse button to activate selection usually will be quicker,
as long as you have a mouse.

The Currency format you selected here is the same one you applied to
the Checks column using the Style drop-down list box.

For now, you have nothing to enter in the Deposits column, and, since
the Balance values will be calculated by the program, you can leave that
column blank also.

Entering the Check Numbers

The Reference column will hold transaction numbers for checks
and deposits. You don't need to apply any special formatting to this

column, since the default (Normal) will work just fine. Enter the check numbers now.

1. Drag the pointer to highlight the range **B4:B8**.

2. Type the check-number data, pressing ↵ after each entry:

721

722

723

724

725

Labeling the Last Row

Before you end this work session, add a label to the last row, which will hold the totals of the columns that hold currency amounts.

1. Select the cell **A10**.

2. Type **Totals** and press ↵.

Your sheet should now look like this:

	A	B	C	D	E	F	G	H	I
1									
2	Date	Reference	Checks	Deposits	Balance				
3									
4	1/3/95	721	$15.95						
5	1/5/95	722	$64.35						
6	1/6/95	723	$21.50						
7	1/6/95	724	$40.00						
8	1/6/95	725	$103.12						
9									
10	Totals		$244.92						
11									
12									

CHECK.XLS

You have nearly completed the layout of the check register. In the next session, you will complete the layout. You will also add formulas, or pre-defined calculations, to the sheet so that it can actually generate a checkbook balance.

Saving Your Work

Always save your work at the end of a session. Since you've already named the worksheet file CHECK.XLS, you don't need to use the File ➤ Save As command to assign a name. You can save the file in a single step:

- From the **File** pull-down menu, select **Save**.

The updated file will be written to disk, replacing the previous version of CHECK.XLS. You can now end the session and exit Excel.

3 Developing a a Running Balance

In this lesson, you will edit the check register you created in Lessons 1 and 2. The completed worksheet will be able to maintain a running balance as you enter transaction items.

To begin this session, restart Excel and open the file CHECK.XLS.

Providing for a Starting Balance

You must have a place to enter the starting account balance from which check amounts will be deducted and deposits will be added. Follow these steps:

1. Click cell **D3**.

2. Type the label **Balance forward** --> and press ↵.

> **● Note** Use two hyphens (--) followed by a greater-than symbol (>) in your label entry in step 2. The purpose is to provide a graphic pointer to cell E3, which will hold the starting balance amount.

3. In the toolbar, click the **Right Align** tool.

Quick&Easy

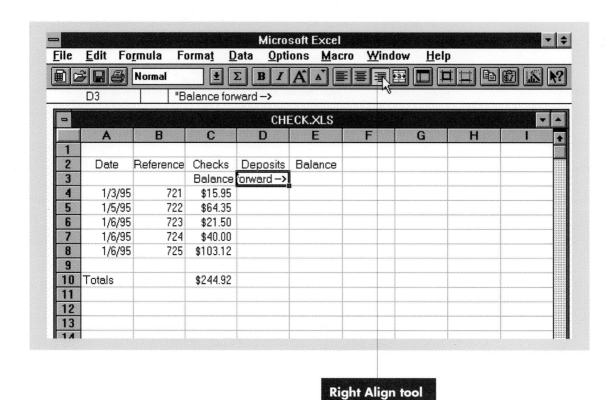

Right Align tool

Now apply the proper number format to the cell that will hold the
starting balance.

4. Click cell **E3**.

5. Select **Currency** from the Style drop-down list box in the
toolbar.

Entering Formulas That Calculate the Running Balance

For the check register to be useful, it must maintain a running balance of the account. This can be done by way of *formulas,* or built-in calculations.

In Excel, a formula is a special type of cell entry that defines a calculation, usually in relation to other cells. Much of the power and convenience of programs like Excel comes from the ability to embed formulas in worksheets.

Actually, you already entered one formula into the sheet when you used the AutoSum tool. To view the formula, click cell C10. The formula appears above the top of the sheet in the formula bar:

=SUM(C4:C9)

An Excel formula always begins with an equal sign (=). In the example, SUM is a *function,* or built-in type of calculation. SUM is the function for the arithmetic operation of addition.

The identifiers enclosed in parentheses show which cells will be operated on by the function. In the example, it is all the cells in the range

C4:C9 (the Checks column). So, a formula that does not use the SUM function but produces the same result would be

=C4+C5+C6+C7+C8+C9

Enter a formula now that will calculate the checkbook balance.

1. Click cell **E4**.

2. Type the formula =**E3−C4+D4**.

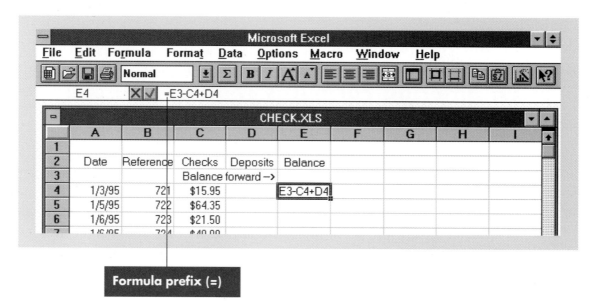

Formula prefix (=)

3. Press ↵.

This formula takes the starting balance (cell E3), subtracts the check amount in C4, and adds any deposit amount in D4. When you press ↵ after entering the formula, its result (a data value) will appear in the cell. (Blank cells are treated as zeros.)

You could enter a formula into each cell of column E to calculate the balance at each point. However, there's an easier way to do this.

4. With cell E4 still highlighted, click the **Copy** tool in the toolbar (the fourth button from the right). This copies the contents of the selected cell to the Windows Clipboard, a temporary storage area.

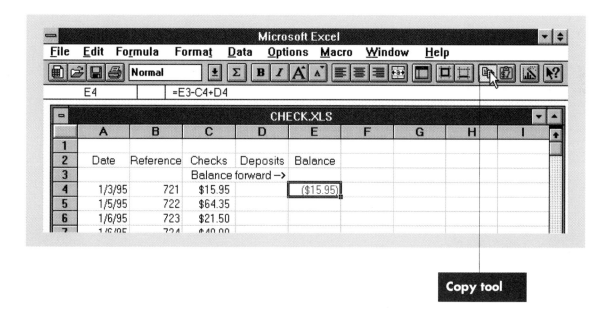

Copy tool

A moving dotted line surrounds the selected cell.

5. Drag the cell pointer from cell **E5** to cell **E9**, highlighting the range E5:E9.

	A	B	C	D	E	F	G	H	I
1									
2	Date	Reference	Checks	Deposits	Balance				
3			Balance forward →						
4	1/3/95	721	$15.95		($15.95)				
5	1/5/95	722	$64.35						
6	1/6/95	723	$21.50						
7	1/6/95	724	$40.00						
8	1/6/95	725	$103.12						
9									
10	Totals		$244.92						
11									
12									
13									

Drag from here...

...to here.

6. Press ↵.

● **Note** The Copy operation is an example of how Excel provides several alternatives for doing the same thing. Selecting the Copy tool in step 4 produces the same result as selecting Edit ➤ Copy (or Copy from the shortcut menu). And pressing ↵ in step 6 is the same as selecting Edit ➤ Paste—it pastes one copy of the formula into each cell of the selected range. Use the procedure that is most comfortable for you. When you are using a mouse, you will probably prefer using the Copy command from the shortcut menu or clicking the Copy tool. Use Edit ➤ Copy mainly from the keyboard.

Notice also that Excel has adjusted the cell references in the pasted formulas. For example, when you finish the procedure, the contents of cell E5 is shown in the formula bar:

=E4−C5+D5

In this formula, the cell references E3, C4, and D4 of the original formula have been adjusted automatically by the program to E4, C5, and D5. If you click other cells in the range, you will find that the formula has been readjusted in each cell.

This is an important feature of Excel:

> **The program can readjust cell references when a formula is copied or moved within a sheet so that its result is still valid.**

Summing the Deposits

You don't yet have any entries in the Deposits column, but you will want to be able to provide for a total of deposits.

You could click cell D10 and use the AutoSum tool, just as you did in the Checks column. Here's an opportunity, however, to use a new feature of Excel 4.0 for Windows, AutoFill. The AutoFill feature copies the contents of a cell into adjacent cells—just by dragging. The result is the same as using the Copy tool, except the cells must always be adjacent to one another.

Here's how AutoFill works. The formula you need in cell D10 to generate the total of the Deposits column is the same as the one in

Quick & Easy

C10—except that the cell references need to be readjusted. If you copy the formula in C10 into D10, the program will take care of the readjustment.

1. Click cell **C10**.

2. While the cell is highlighted, move the cell pointer to the bottom-right corner of the cell (the *fill handle*). The pointer will change to a solid plus sign.

	A	B	C	D	E	F	G	H	I
					CHECK.XLS				
1									
2	Date	Reference	Checks	Deposits	Balance				
3			Balance forward –>						
4	1/3/95	721	$15.95		($15.95)				
5	1/5/95	722	$64.35		($80.30)				
6	1/6/95	723	$21.50		($101.80)				
7	1/6/95	724	$40.00		($141.80)				
8	1/6/95	725	$103.12		($244.92)				
9					($244.92)				
10	Totals		$244.92						
11									
12									

AutoFill pointer

3. Drag the + pointer one cell to the right until the highlight includes both cells **C10** and **D10**.

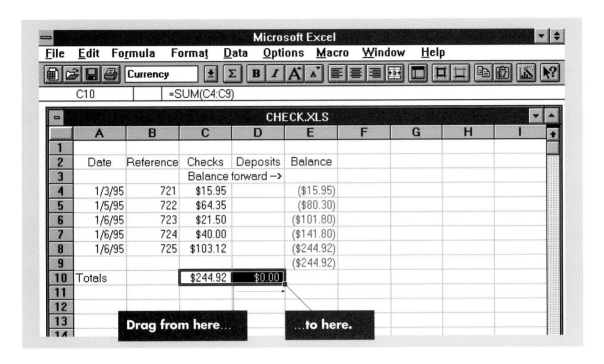

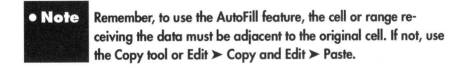

Now, if you click cell D10, you will see its contents above the sheet in the formula bar:

=SUM(D4:D9)

This is precisely the formula you need to generate the Deposits total, and the program derived it from the Checks total formula in C10, just as expected.

> **● Note** Remember, to use the AutoFill feature, the cell or range re-
> ceiving the data must be adjacent to the original cell. If not, use
> the Copy tool or Edit ➤ Copy and Edit ➤ Paste.

Entering a Formula for the Current Balance

The current checkbook balance will be shown in column E on the line of the last transaction entered. However, to assure the accuracy of this

Quick&Easy

electronic check register, it would be a good idea to provide another way of developing the balance. In accounting terms, this is similar to the practice of *cross-footing* a manual spreadsheet. That is, the sum of the columns should equal the sum of the rows: You should be able to get the same grand total by adding either down or across the sheet.

In the case of the check register, you should be able to calculate the balance by subtracting the total in the Checks column (cell C10) from the starting balance in E3 and adding any deposits (D10). A formula for this calculation would be

$$=E3-C10+D10$$

Enter this formula into the sheet now.

1. Click cell **E10**.

2. Type the formula =E3−C10+D10.

	Microsoft Excel								
File	**Edit**	**Formula**	**Format**	**Data**	**Options**	**Macro**	**Window**	**Help**	

				Normal	Σ	B	I	A	A								

E10   X ✓ =E3-C10+D10

	CHECK.XLS								
	A	B	C	D	E	F	G	H	I
1									
2	Date	Reference	Checks	Deposits	Balance				
3			Balance forward →						
4	1/3/95	721	$15.95		($15.95)				
5	1/5/95	722	$64.35		($80.30)				
6	1/6/95	723	$21.50		($101.80)				
7	1/6/95	724	$40.00		($141.80)				
8	1/6/95	725	$103.12		($244.92)				
9					($244.92)				
10	Totals		$244.92	$0.00	=C10+D10				
11									
12									
13									

3. Press ↵.

Putting the Worksheet to Work!

By now, you've provided all the formulas required to calculate the check register. Enter a starting balance of $1,000, enter a deposit item of $250 on 1/6/95, and let Excel do the rest.

1. Click cell **E3**.

2. Type the starting balance: **1000**.

3. Press ↵.

4. Click cell **D6**.

5. Type the deposit amount: **250**.

6. Press ↵.

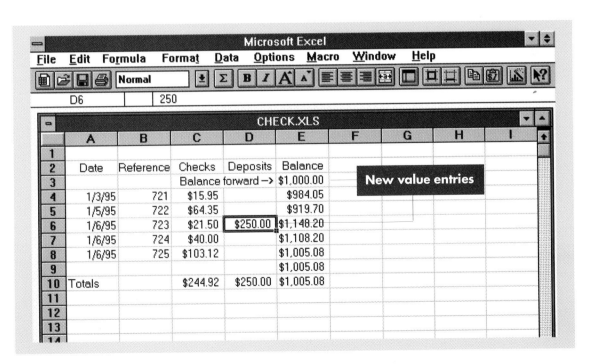

Each time you make a data entry in the check register, the program updates the totals and balance.

This check register, although functional, lacks a feature that would make it truly convenient: It should be possible for the check listing to grow (as you add more items and rows) so that an ongoing register can be maintained.

Expanding the Sheet

One of the difficulties in expanding the sheet lies in the way it has been designed. The Totals row limits addition of check listings. One solution is to put the Totals row on *top* of the sheet.

Moving a Row Using Drag-and-Drop

Move the Totals row now using the *drag-and-drop* method.

1. Select the range **A10:E10**.

2. Move the pointer to any edge of the highlighted range until its shape changes to an arrow.

	A	B	C	D	E	F	G	H	I
				CHECK.XLS					
1									
2	Date	Reference	Checks	Deposits	Balance				
3			Balance forward –>		$1,000.00				
4	1/3/95	721	$15.95		$984.05				
5	1/5/95	722	$64.35		$919.70				
6	1/6/95	723	$21.50	$250.00	$1,148.20				
7	1/6/95	724	$40.00		$1,108.20				
8	1/6/95	725	$103.12		$1,005.08				
9					$1,005.08				
10	Totals		$244.92	$250.00	$1,005.08				
11									
12									

**Move arrow
(at border of cell highlight).**

3. Click and hold the mouse button. Keep holding the button down as you drag the row up into the range **A1:E1**. (An outline of the range will move with the pointer.)

4. Release the mouse button.

	A	B	C	D	E	F	G	H	I
1	Totals		$244.92	$250.00	$1,005.08				
2	Date	Reference	Checks	Deposits	Balance	↑		**...to here.**	
3			Balance forward –>		$1,000.00				
4	1/3/95	721	$15.95		$984.05				
5	1/5/95	722	$64.35		$919.70				
6	1/6/95	723	$21.50	$250.00	$1,148.20				
7	1/6/95	724	$40.00		$1,108.20				
8	1/6/95	725	$103.12		$1,005.08				
9					$1,005.08			**Drag from here...**	
10									
11									
12									

CHECK.XLS

Formatting the Rest of the Sheet

Notice that row 9 has no data entries but includes the Balance formula. It is always good practice to leave a blank, formatted row so that you can copy it to expand the sheet.

1. Select the range **A9:E9**.

2. Move the cell pointer to the bottom-right corner of the cell until it changes to a solid plus sign.

3. Drag the + pointer downward and *off the bottom of the sheet* at E18, as you continue to hold down the mouse button. The display will begin to scroll.

Quick&Easy

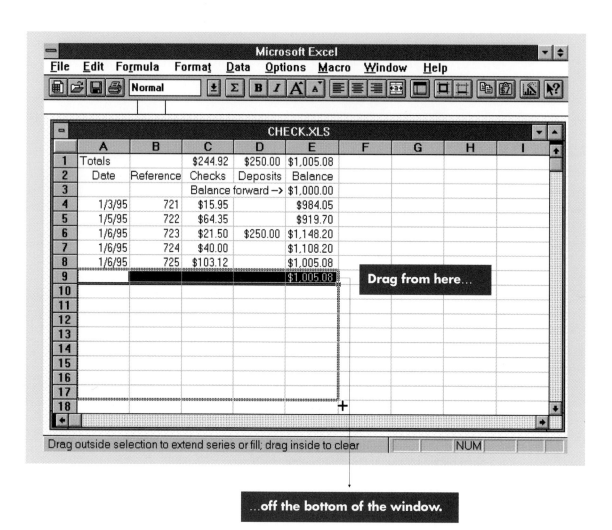

4. Keep holding down the button as the rows scroll past.
   Release the mouse button at row 100.

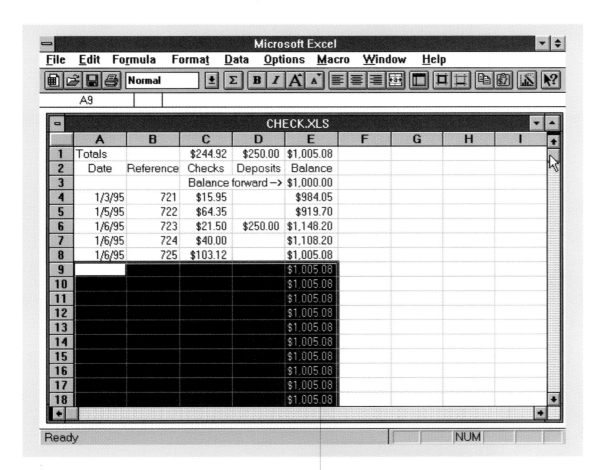

Drag the fill handle off the bottom of the window, and the sheet will scroll.

By pasting the formulas from the blank row into the rest of the sheet, you have provided for as many entries as you specified rows in step 4. If you run out of room, you can always repeat this procedure. To make

43

it easy to expand the sheet later, be sure to leave one blank row that can be used for copying.

Going to the Top of the Sheet

The cell pointer should now be at cell E100. In preparation for the next series of steps:

1. Drag the scroll box upward in the scroll bar at the right side of the window. This will scroll the display back toward the top of the sheet.

2. Release the mouse button when the scroll box is at the very top of the range. The Totals row should be displayed.

Editing the Formulas

Even though the program readjusted the formulas when you moved the Totals row, the formulas that generate the Checks and Deposits totals don't now include all the new cells in the sheet. Edit the formulas to include the new cells.

1. Click cell **C1**. The formula for the total of the Checks column appears in the formula bar:

=SUM(C4:C9)

2. Move the pointer into the formula bar. Its shape changes to the I-beam cursor.

3. Drag the I-beam over the digit 9 to highlight it.

Drag to highlight the portion of the entry to be replaced.

4. Type the replacement value: **100**.

5. Press ↵.

6. Repeat steps 1–5 in cell D1 to change its formula to read =SUM(D4:D100)

Splitting the Window

The check register now includes enough rows for 97 transaction items (100 rows minus the first 3). However, as the listing grows, it will become inconvenient to keep scrolling between the bottom and the top. Excel has a handy solution for this.

1. Click cell **A4**.

2. From the **Window** pull-down menu, select **Split**.

Quick&Easy

	File	Edit	Formula	Format	Data	Options	Macro	**Window**	Help

Microsoft Excel

Normal Σ **B** *I* **A** Δ ≡ ≡

New Window
Arrange...
Hide
Unhide...
View...

Split
Freeze Panes
Zoom...

✓ **1 CHECK.XLS**
2 Sheet1

A4   1/3/1995

CHECK.XLS

	A	B	C	D	E		H	I
1	Totals		$244.92	$250.00	$1,005.08			
2	Date	Reference	Checks	Deposits	Balance			
3			Balance forward →		$1,000.00			
4	1/3/95	721	$15.95		$984.05			
5	1/5/95	722	$64.35		$919.70			
6	1/6/95	723	$21.50	$250.00	$1,148.20			
7	1/6/95	724	$40.00		$1,108.20			
8	1/6/95	725	$103.12		$1,005.08			
9					$1,005.08			
10					$1,005.08			
11					$1,005.08			
12					$1,005.08			
13					$1,005.08			
14					$1,005.08			
15					$1,005.08			
16					$1,005.08			
17					$1,005.08			
18					$1,005.08			

Split window at active cell   NUM

**In step 1, select
the row for splitting.**

**In step 2, select
Window ➤ Split.**

Selecting Window ➤ Split creates two separate views of the same sheet,
split just above the selected cell (A4, in this case). You can move the cell
pointer and adjust the scroll boxes separately to adjust the view in each
window. To use the check register, adjust the scroll box in the vertical
scroll bar in the lower window to advance to new transaction-entry
rows. As you do this, the first three rows of the sheet (including Totals) will remain stationary on top.

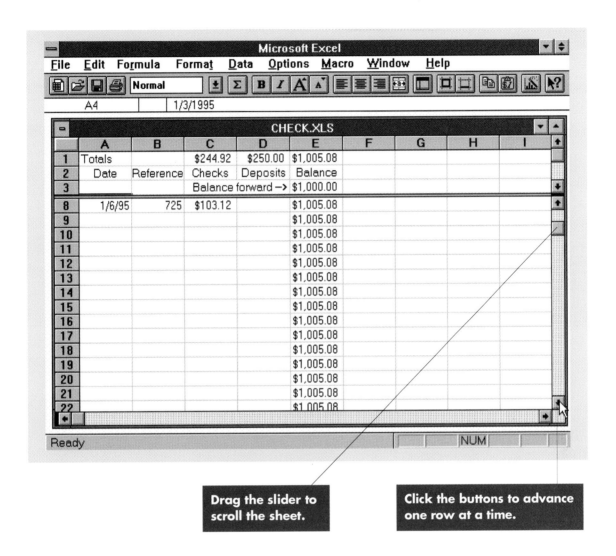

Drag the slider to scroll the sheet.

Click the buttons to advance one row at a time.

To scroll the display, do either of the following:

- Drag the scroll box in the vertical scroll bar to move through large portions of the sheet.

- Click the arrow buttons at either end of the scroll bar to adjust the display one row at a time, up or down.

For example, click the bottom arrow button once to advance the display by one row.

> **• Note** You can remove the split whenever the sheet is open by selecting Window ➤ Remove Split.

Using the Check Register

You now have a fully workable check register!

Remember to leave a blank row at the bottom so that you can expand the sheet quickly and easily to hold more transactions. If you expand the sheet, adjust the formulas that generate totals of checks and deposits. Notice that the repeating totals in column E indicate the extent of unused, but valid, rows. If you come to a row that shows no balance, it contains no formulas and *cannot hold valid entries.* Expand the sheet and readjust the formulas before you enter more transactions.

When you have filled the sheet with one month's transactions, it will be time to open another copy of the sheet to begin the next month. You'll learn how to do this in Lesson 9.

Saving Your Work

Conclude this session—and preserve the check register for your ongoing use—by saving CHECK.XLS to disk.

> **• Note** If you save the sheet when split, the split view will appear when you reopen the file. And the cell pointer will be located just where it was when the file was saved, ready for you to resume work!

1. Select **File** ➤ **Save**.

2. Select **File** ➤ **Exit** to quit Excel.

4

15 MINUTES

Designing an Expense Report

In this lesson, you will use the skills you picked up in the first part of this book to create a new worksheet, an employee expense report. You will find that the steps to set up the sheet and its formulas are similar to the ones you took to create the check register. However, this time you will also discover some new techniques that can help make it quick and easy for you to do even more ambitious projects.

To begin this lesson, start Excel (if you need help, refer to Lesson 1). You'll see the empty document window named Sheet1:

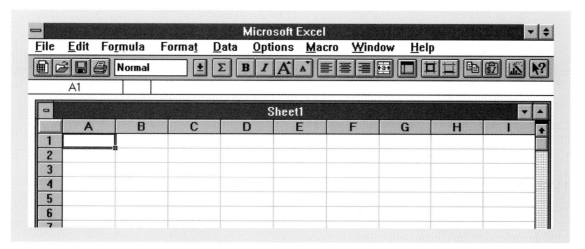

Entering a Title, Text, and Column Headings

Start to lay out the sheet by entering some descriptive text labels.

1. Click cell **C1**.

2. Type the sheet title: **Monthly Expense Report** and press ↵.

File	Edit	Formula	Format	Data	Options	Macro	Window	Help

Microsoft Excel

Normal

C1   'Monthly Expense Report

Sheet1

	A	B	C	D	E	F	G	H	I
1			Monthly Expense Report						
2									

3. Click cell **A2**.

4. Type **Name:** and press ↵.

5. Click cell **D2**.

6. Type **Department:** and press ↵.

7. Click cell **G2**.

8. Type **Date:** and press ↵.

G2   'Date:

Sheet1

	A	B	C	D	E	F	G	H	I
1			Monthly Expense Report						
2	Name:			Department:			Date:		
3									
4									
5									
6									

You now need to select the row A3:H3 in preparation for entering the column headings. Discover one of the new features of Excel 4.0 for Windows—AutoSelect—by making the selection as described below.

9. While holding down Shift, double-click the *right edge* of cell A3. The entire row A3:H3 will be selected to receive your data entry.

● Note The AutoSelect feature extends your selection to the edge of the sheet. Double-clicking the right edge of a cell while holding down Shift selects all the cells in the row to the right that contain data, to the end of the row. Double-clicking the *bottom* edge of a cell while holding down Shift selects all the cells in the column below that contain data. These AutoSelect procedures have the same effect as dragging the cell pointer from the first to the last cell in the desired range. Use the method that you find the most convenient.

10. Type the following column headings, pressing ↵ after each item: **Date, Description, Transport, Lodging, Meals, Misc, Totals,** and **Account.**

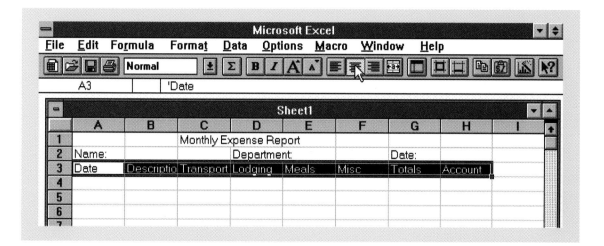

Quick Easy

11. With A3:H3 still selected, click the **Center Align** tool to center the headings over the columns.

Adjusting the Column Width

Note that the Description entry in cell B3 is so long that it overflows its cell. Make an adjustment now to fix that.

1. Move the pointer into the sheet column headings, and position it on the boundary between columns B and C. The pointer shape will change to a double arrow.

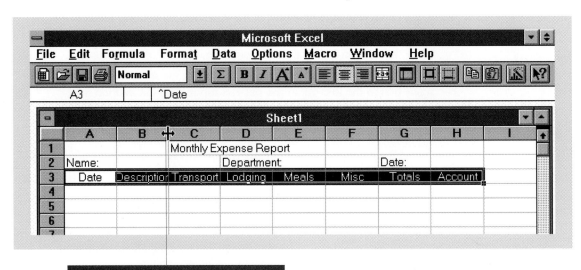

The pointer changes shape when you move it to a boundary in the column headings.

2. Drag the double-arrow pointer—and the column border with it—to the right.

3. Release the mouse button when the column width has been adjusted to match the illustration:

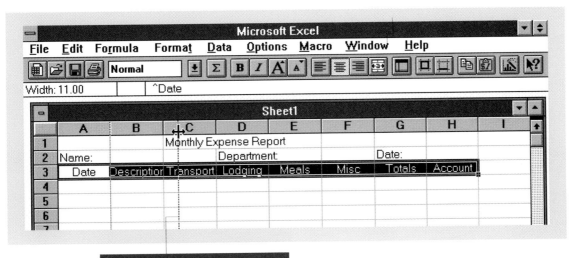

Drag the column boundary to adjust its width.

Adding the Remaining Text Labels

There are just three more text labels required for this sheet. Enter them now.

1. Click cell **A14**.

2. Type **Totals** and press ↵.

3. Drag the pointer from cell **F15** to cell **F16** to highlight F15:F16.

4. Type **Less advances** and press ↵.

5. Type **Amount owed you** and press ↵.

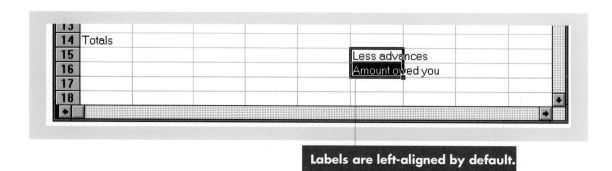

Labels are left-aligned by default.

6. With F15:F16 still selected, click the **Right Align** tool.

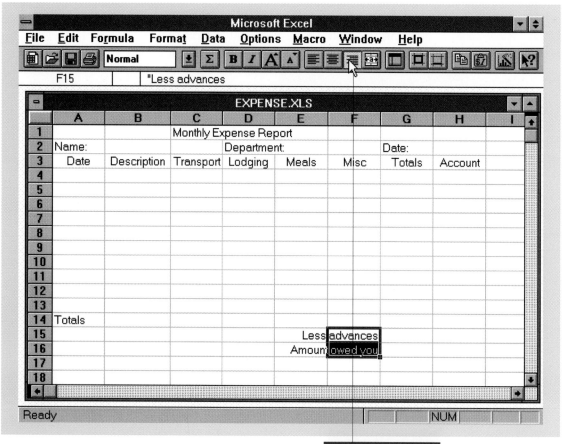

Right Align tool

The labels in F15 and F16 are now right-aligned to be flush with the values that will appear in cells G15 and G16.

Applying Data Formats

You have completed the basic layout of the expense report form. To provide for accurate displays, apply data formats now to the columns that will hold dates and currency amounts.

1. Select the range **A4:A13**.

2. Click the right mouse button to activate a shortcut menu.

3. From the menu, select **Number**.

The Number Format dialog box will open.

4. In the Category list box, select **Date**.

Quick Easy

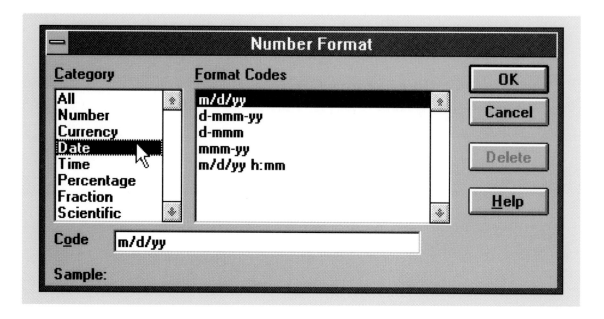

5. The default format code (*m/d/yy*) is suitable, so simply select **OK** to accept the entries and close the dialog box.

6. Select the range **C4:G14**.

There are two other cells in the sheet that must be formatted the same way as the range you have selected. You can add them to the selection—and therefore perform all the required formatting at the same time. Do this now.

7. While holding down **Ctrl**, click cells **G15** and **G16**. These cells will be added to your range selection.

8. Click the right mouse button to activate a shortcut menu.

9. From the menu, select **Number**.

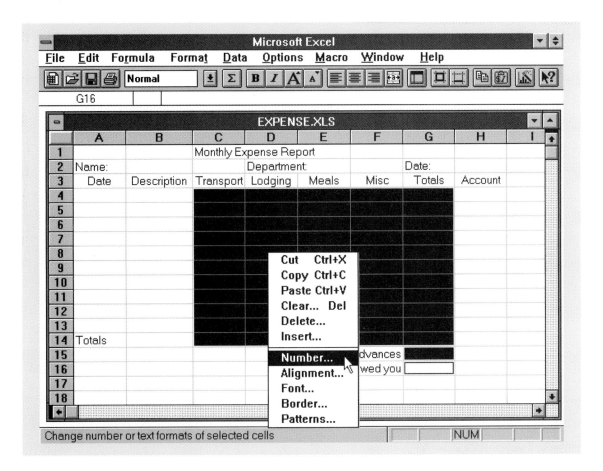

The Number Format dialog box will open.

10. In the Category list box, select **Currency**.

11. In the Format Code list box, select the third format from the top (thousands separator with pennies).

Quick&Easy

Number Format

Category	Format Codes	
All	$#,##0_);($#,##0)	**OK**
Number	$#,##0_);[Red]($#,##0)	**Cancel**
Currency	**$#,##0.00_);($#,##0.00)**	
Date	$#,##0.00_);[Red]($#,##0.00)	**Delete**
Time		
Percentage		**Help**
Fraction		
Scientific		

Code $#,##0.00_);($#,##0.00)

Sample:

**Currency format with thousands separator (,) and pennies
Example: $5,000.00**

12. Select **OK** to accept the entries and close the dialog box.

Saving Your Work So Far

Although you haven't finished this lesson yet, you have done a significant amount of work. It is good practice to save your work not only at the conclusion of each lesson but also at intermediate points to prevent losing data due to accidents, such as disruptions of electrical power.

This time, use a feature on the toolbar as an alternative to the File ➤ Save command.

1. From the toolbar, select the **Save** tool, the third button from the left.

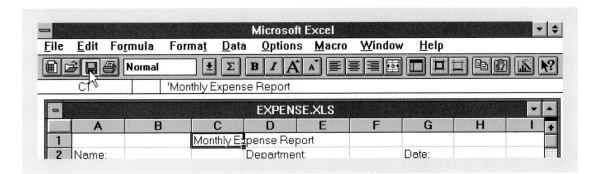

Since this is the first time you have saved this sheet and you have not yet given it a unique name, the Save As dialog box will appear.

2. Type **expense**.

3. Press ↵.

> **● Note** When you enter a new file name, you can omit the extension.
> The program will add the correct Excel worksheet extension
> (.XLS) automatically. (The option Save File As Type in the Save
> As dialog box must be set to Normal, the default.)

Defining Range Names

Recall that a notation with two cell addresses linked by a colon speci-
fies a worksheet range. This is the method used to specify ranges in the
formulas you included in the check register. However, specifying ranges
by explicit addresses can become tedious, especially as you begin to
build and edit larger sheets. Furthermore, the addresses in a range reference are simply locations and tell you nothing about the range itself. It
would be convenient to have a more meaningful way of specifying
ranges.

An alternative method of specifying ranges is to give them names,
much as you would name a variable in an algebra problem. You can
then insert the name of a range in formulas rather than specify the addresses. This is usually more convenient and—perhaps more important—makes the formulas in your sheet more understandable. This
way, if you must revise a sheet you haven't used in a while, you will
have little difficulty understanding its formulas at a glance.

Now, name some of the ranges in the Expense sheet in preparation for
entering formulas.

1. Select the range **C4:C13**.

2. From the menu bar, select Formula ➤ Define Name.

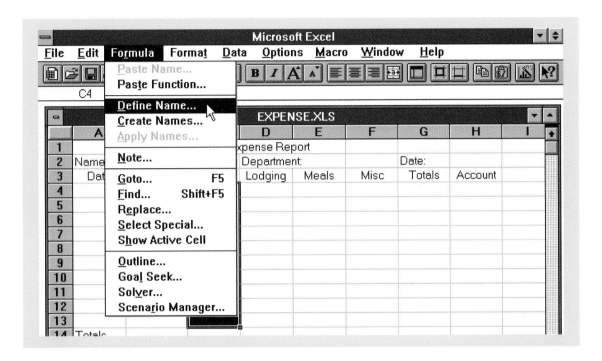

The Define Name dialog box will appear. In the dialog box, note that the column heading of the selected range appears in the Name text box, and the addresses of its cell boundaries appear in the Refers To box.

3. To accept these values, simply click the **Add** button.

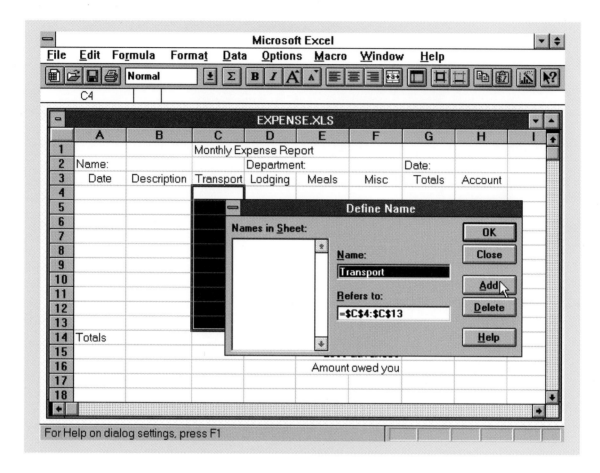

4. The range name *Transport* will now appear in the Names In Sheet list box. Select **OK** to close the dialog box.

5. Repeat steps 1–4 for each of the following ranges and names: **D4:D13** (Lodging), **E4:E13** (Meals), and **F4:F13** (Misc).

A range can be a single cell, so individual cells also can have range names. This will come in handy for two other cells in the sheet.

6. Select cell **G14**.

7. From the menu bar, select **Formula ➤ Define Name**. The Define Name dialog box will appear.

8. Type **total** in the Name text box.

9. Select the **OK** button.

10. Repeat steps 6–9 to select cell **G15** and name it **advances**.

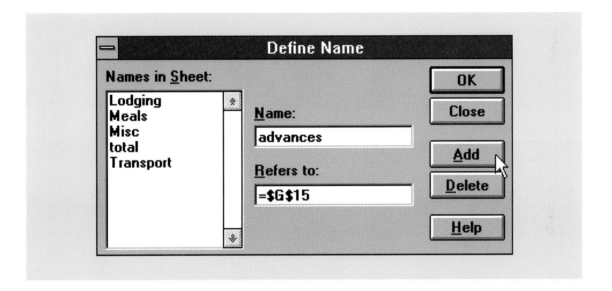

Entering Formulas into the Sheet

In Lesson 1, you used the AutoSum tool to specify formulas for arithmetic totals. Now that you have named each of the columns of expense categories in this sheet, you have an alternative way of developing the totals. Follow these steps to see how you can use range names in formulas:

1. Select cell **C14**.

2. Type **=sum(transport)**.

Quick Easy

```
 ┌──────────────────────────────────────────────────────────────────┐
 │ ─                        Microsoft Excel                    ▼ ▼   │
 ├──────────────────────────────────────────────────────────────────┤
 │ File   Edit  Formula   Format   Data   Options   Macro   Window   Help │
 ├──────────────────────────────────────────────────────────────────┤
 │ [icons] Normal  ▼ Σ  B  I  A  A  ≡ ≡ ≡ ≣ □ □ □ ▣ ▨ ▨ ▶? │
 ├──────────────────────────────────────────────────────────────────┤
 │    C14          │     =SUM(Transport)                              │
 └──────────────────────────────────────────────────────────────────┘
```

	A	B	C	D	E	F	G	H	I
1			Monthly Expense Report						
2	Name:			Department:			Date:		
3	Date	Description	Transport	Lodging	Meals	Misc	Totals	Account	
4									
5									
6									
7									
8									
9									
10									
11									
12									
13									
14	Totals		$0.00						
15					Less advances				
16					Amount owed you				
17									
18									

Ready

Recall that an Excel formula always begins with an equal sign (=).
In cell C14, you entered a formula that contains the SUM function,
which is a built-in formula for the arithmetic operation of addition.
This time, instead of cell addresses, the identifier enclosed in parentheses is the range name.

The program simply substitutes the corresponding cell addresses each time it encounters a range name. For example, using the range name in this formula is the same as entering

=SUM(C4:C13)

And using the SUM function is the same as entering each cell in the calculation

=C4+C5+C6+C7+C8+C9+C10+C11+C12+C13

Another advantage of using a range name is that you need not keep track of addresses if you move the range or otherwise edit the sheet. The program will adjust the cell addresses as necessary, and the range name will be unchanged.

Entering Formulas for the Other Expense Categories

Use the range names you already defined in formulas for the totals of the other expense categories.

1. Select cell **D14**.

2. Type **=sum(lodging)** and press ↵.

3. In **E14**, type **=sum(meals)** and press ↵.

4. In **F14**, type **=sum(misc)** and press ↵.

Quick Easy

```
┌─────────────────────────────────────────────────────────────────────┐
│ ─                        Microsoft Excel                        ▼ ⬍  │
│  File  Edit  Formula  Format  Data  Options  Macro  Window  Help    │
│ ┌──┬──┬──┬──┐┌────────┐┌──┬─┬───┬───┬───┐┌──┬──┬──┬─┐┌──┬──┬──┬──┬──┐│
│ │  │  │  │  ││ Normal ││ ±│Σ│ B │ I │ A ││  │  │  │ ││  │  │  │  │ ▶?││
│ └──┴──┴──┴──┘└────────┘└──┴─┴───┴───┴───┘└──┴──┴──┴─┘└──┴──┴──┴──┴──┘│
│      F14          │      =SUM(Misc)                                  │
│ ┌───────────────────────────────────────────────────────────────┐   │
│ │ ─                      EXPENSE.XLS                        ▼ ▲  │   │
│ │      A        B         C        D       E       F       G        H       I │
│ │  1                   Monthly Expense Report                          │
│ │  2  Name:                        Department:          Date:          │
│ │  3   Date   Description Transport Lodging  Meals    Misc   Totals  Account │
│ │  4                                                                   │
│ │  5                                                                   │
│ │  6                                                                   │
│ │  7                                                                   │
│ │  8                                                                   │
│ │  9                                                                   │
│ │ 10                                                                   │
│ │ 11                                                                   │
│ │ 12                                                                   │
│ │ 13                                                                   │
│ │ 14  Totals              $0.00    $0.00   $0.00   $0.00               │
│ │ 15                                       Less advances               │
│ │ 16                                       Amount owed you             │
│ │ 17                                                                   │
│ │ 18                                                                   │
│ └───────────────────────────────────────────────────────────────┘   │
│ Ready                                                                 │
└─────────────────────────────────────────────────────────────────────┘
```

Providing for the Row Totals

You want to sum the entries across the form, by row, as well as down the form, by column. On an expense report, the row totals typically represent daily expenditures in all categories. In the following steps, you will use the AutoSum tool to generate the basic formula, then use AutoFill to apply the formula to all the rows in the sheet.

1. Select cell **G4**.

2. Click the **AutoSum** tool.

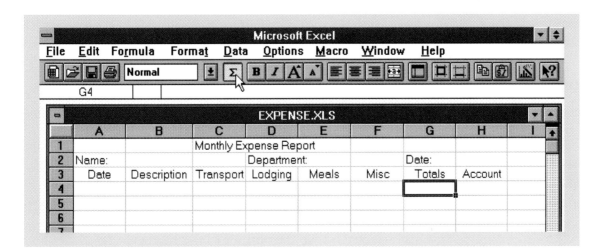

3. Drag the pointer from **C4** to **F4** so that the dotted-line reference box surrounds the range C4:F4.

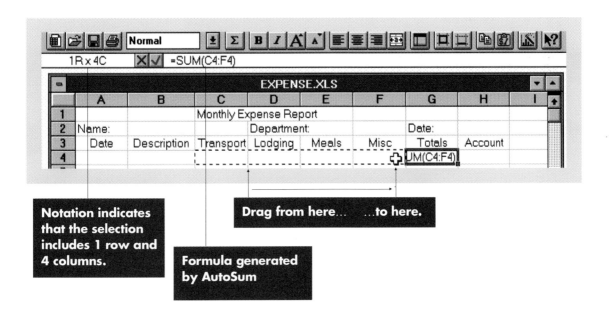

Notation indicates that the selection includes 1 row and 4 columns.

Formula generated by AutoSum

Drag from here...   ...to here.

Note that the AutoSum tool generated the following formula and inserted it in the selected cell (G4):

=SUM(C4:F4).

Recall from Lesson 3 that you can use the AutoFill feature to copy this
formula to adjacent ranges in the sheet. Do this now to copy the formula into the rest of the cells in the Totals column. As you do so, the
program will adjust the cell addresses so that they refer to the correct
row in each instance.

1. With cell G4 still selected, move the pointer to the fill handle (in the bottom-right corner of the cell highlight). The
pointer shape will change to a solid plus sign.

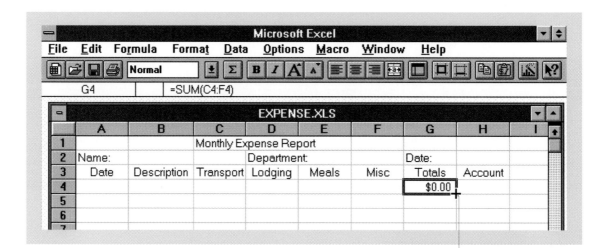

When you move the
pointer to the fill
handle, it changes
to the + shape.

2. Drag the fill handle from cell **G4** to cell **G14**.

	Date	Description	Transport	Lodging	Meals	Misc	Totals	Account	
3	Date	Description	Transport	Lodging	Meals	Misc	Totals	Account	
4							$0.00		**Drag from here…**
5									
6									
7									
8									
9									
10									
11									
12									
13									
14	Totals		$0.00	$0.00	$0.00	$0.00			**…to here.**
15					Less advances				
16					Amount owed you				

Calculating the Reimbursement Amount

You have one more formula to enter into this sheet, which will calculate the amount of your reimbursement. Since you have already assigned names to the ranges required, you can insert them in the formula.

1. Select cell **G16**.

2. Type =**total-advances**.

Quick&Easy

This formula performs arithmetic subtraction. The minus sign (−) indicates that the amount in cell G15 (Advances) will be subtracted from the amount in cell G14 (Total). The result is your net cash outlay, or Amount Owed You, which will be displayed in cell G16.

Saving the Completed Worksheet Layout

You have completed all the steps required to create a fully functional worksheet that will report expenses and calculate the amount of cash reimbursement to you.

Before ending this lesson, be sure to save your work. Since you already named the worksheet file in the previous Save As operation, you can save it now in a single action by pressing a shortcut key combination.

1. Hold down **Shift** while you press **F12**. The updated sheet will be saved to the file EXPENSE.XLS.

2. You can exit Excel by using another shortcut key combination: Hold down **Alt** while you press **F4**.

● Note Shortcut keys are available as convenient alternatives for some of the more commonly used commands from the pull-down menus. Pressing Shift-F12 has the same effect as selecting File ➤ Save or clicking the Save tool. Pressing Alt-F4 is the same as selecting File ➤ Exit. Use the method that is most comfortable for you.

In the next lesson you will enter data into the sheet and work on its appearance.

Formatting the Expense Report

5

In Lesson 4, you designed an employee expense report, including laying out the sheet and embedding calculations as formulas. When you designed the sheet, you applied *number formats* to certain columns to cause them to be displayed properly as dates or as currency amounts.

In this lesson, you will learn about some other types of formatting that affect the appearance of the worksheet. You will also learn how to use the expense form as a *template*, or model, for generating monthly expense reports.

Opening the Expense Sheet

Once you have restarted Windows and the Excel application, begin this lesson by reopening the EXPENSE.XLS document file you saved at the conclusion of Lesson 4. As an alternative to selecting File ➤ Open, try another method, which uses a feature of the toolbar.

1. Start Excel.

2. From the toolbar, select the **Open File** tool, the second one from the left.

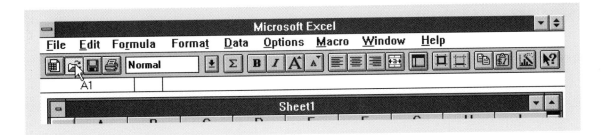

The Open dialog box will appear, with worksheet files in the current directory listed under the File Name box.

3. In the file listing, double-click the name **expense.xls**.

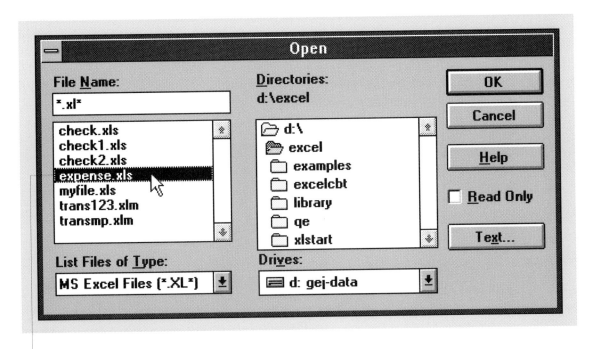

Double-clicking a file name is an alternative to clicking it, then selecting OK.

The sheet will be loaded into an Excel document window.

Quick&Easy

Using AutoFormat

Excel 4.0 for Windows has a new feature called AutoFormat that allows
you to apply predesigned appearance formats to your own worksheets.
Try it now. You must first select the range within the sheet that will be
formatted. Use a variation on the AutoSelect feature you learned in the
previous lesson.

1. Click cell **A3**.

2. While holding down **Shift**, click in cell **H14**.

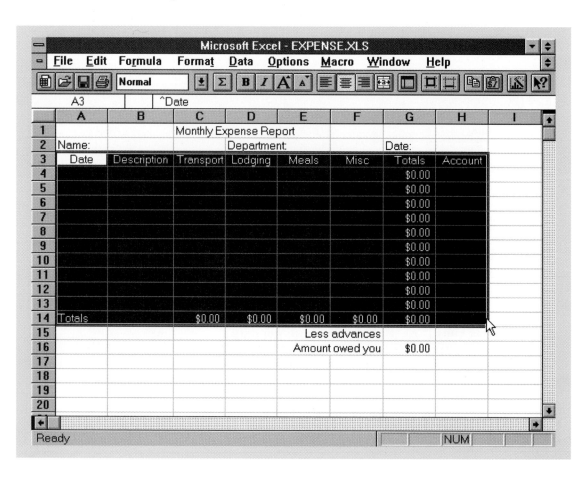

3. With the range highlighted, select **Format ➤ AutoFormat**.

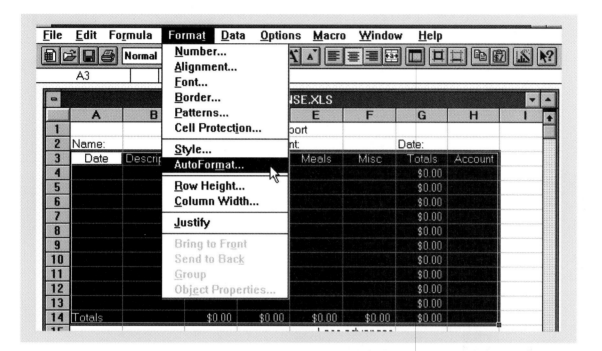

The AutoFormat tool applies the last pre-designed appearance format you used.

The AutoFormat dialog box will appear. Names of predesigned formats are listed in the Table Format box on the left, and a view of the current selection (Classic 1) is displayed in the Sample box on the right.

4. In the Table Format list, click **List 1**. A view of your selection will appear in the Sample box.

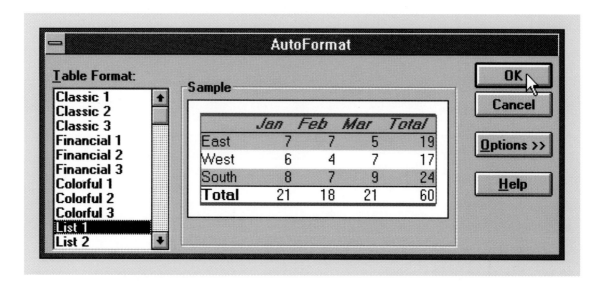

5. Select **OK** to accept the entry and close the dialog box.

> **● Note** If you do not need to see the Sample display, you can simply double-click your selection.

The Expense sheet will appear in the document window, and its appearance will be changed to match the List 1 format. Note that colors are shown in reverse because the selected range is still highlighted.

> **● Note** Excel keeps track of your previous AutoFormat selection. To apply this format again, even in future work sessions, simply select the range and click the AutoFormat tool.

6. To unselect the range, click any cell in the sheet. The newly formatted range now will appear in its true colors.

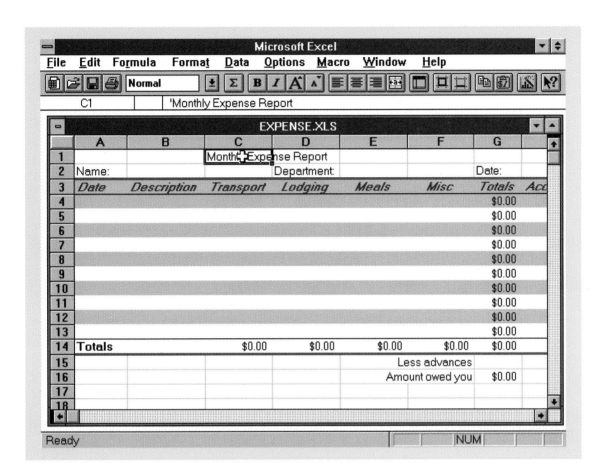

Working with Appearance Formats

Although the program has done much of the appearance formatting, this sheet has some extra items that need individual attention. For one thing, the appearance would be improved further if all the labels matched.

In the next few steps, you will change the formatting of an individual cell. In doing so, you will see how some of the predesigned formatting you applied was created.

1. Click cell **A2**.

2. Click the right mouse button. A shortcut menu will appear.

3. Select **Font**.

The Font dialog box will appear. Within it are a variety of settings that affect the appearance of fonts on the screen. Reset them now to affect the display of cell A2.

4. In the Font Style list, select **Bold Italic**.

5. Click the arrow button of the **Color** drop-down box. A list of colors will appear.

6. From the list of colors, select **Dark Red**.

Font

Font:
MS Sans Serif
MS Sans Serif
■ Black
□ White
▨ Red
▨ Green
■ Blue
□ Yellow
■ Magenta
▨ Cyan
■ Dark Red
■ Dark Green
■ Dark Blue
■ Black

Font Style:
Bold Italic
Regular
Italic
Bold
Bold Italic

Size:
10
10
12
14
15
17

OK
Cancel
☐ Normal Font
Help

Sample

AaBbYyZz

This font style is imitated for the display. The closest matching style will be used for printing.

Step 4

Leave this setting at the default size (10).

In step 5, click the button to open the drop-down box.

Step 6

7. Select **OK** to close the Font dialog box.

The font options for the Name label now match the previously format-ted column headings.

Quick Easy

Copying and Pasting Formats

Now that the appearance of the Name label is the way you want it, you don't have to repeat the process for the rest of the labels you need to change. A quicker way is to copy the formatting of one label to all the others that must match it.

1. If it is not already selected, click cell **A2**.

2. In the toolbar, click the **Copy** tool. A flashing dotted line will appear around the selected cell.

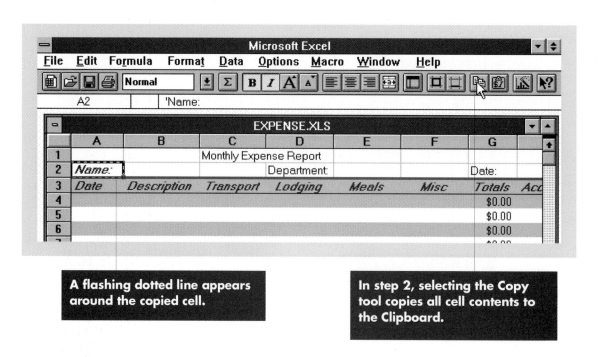

A flashing dotted line appears around the copied cell.

In step 2, selecting the Copy tool copies all cell contents to the Clipboard.

Selecting the Copy tool copies the contents of cell A14, including its data value *and* formatting, to the Clipboard, a temporary memory area of Windows. Now, select the cells that must match the selected cell in appearance.

3. While holding down **Ctrl**, click cells **D2** and **G2**. Your selection now includes both of these cells.

4. In the toolbar, click the **Paste Formats** tool, which is to the right of the Copy tool.

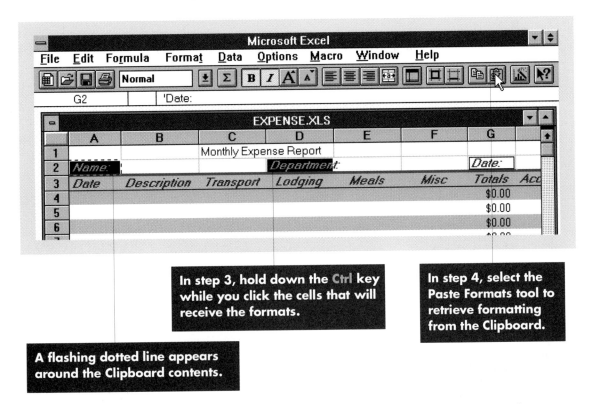

In step 3, hold down the Ctrl key while you click the cells that will receive the formats.

In step 4, select the Paste Formats tool to retrieve formatting from the Clipboard.

A flashing dotted line appears around the Clipboard contents.

The formatting that you copied to the Clipboard will be pasted into the selected cells.

5. Press **Esc** to exit the Paste operation. The flashing dotted line will disappear from cell A2.

Changing Options for a Multiple Selection

Another technique, perhaps faster in some situations, is to select multiple cells or ranges—even if they are not adjacent to one another—then perform a single set of appearance changes. Try this now with the remaining labels in the sheet.

1. While holding down **Ctrl**, click cells **A14**, **F15**, and **F16**.

2. Click the right mouse button to activate a shortcut menu.

3. Select **Font**. The Font dialog box will appear.

4. In the dialog box, make these selections: **Bold Italic** from the Font Style list and **Dark Red** from the Color drop-down list box.

5. Select **OK** to close the dialog box. The text in the selected cells will now be displayed in the new font and color.

	A	B	C	D	E	F	G	
				EXPENSE.XLS				▼ ▲
1			Monthly Expense Report					
2	*Name:*			*Department:*			*Date:*	
3	*Date*	*Description*	*Transport*	*Lodging*	*Meals*	*Misc*	*Totals*	*Acc*
4							$0.00	
5							$0.00	
6							$0.00	
7							$0.00	
8							$0.00	
9							$0.00	
10							$0.00	
11							$0.00	
12							$0.00	
13							$0.00	
14	*Totals*		$0.00	$0.00	$0.00	$0.00	$0.00	
15						*Less advances*		
16						*Amount owed you*	$0.00	
17								
18								▼

Adding Borders

The List 1 table format you applied with the AutoFormat feature includes not only font settings but some other appearance options as well. The ruled lines are types of cell *borders*, and the gray bands are a *shading* option.

> **● Note** When you changed the font options for some of the labels, you may have wondered why you did not simply copy the formatting from the labels in List 1. Formats cannot be copied selectively. If you had copied and pasted the predesigned formatting, the borders and shading would have been copied also. Furthermore, if you move a cell that contains formatting, its formats will move with it. For these reasons, often it will be more convenient to apply an AutoFormat as one of the last steps when you are building a new sheet.

Create a border and shading now that will highlight the Amount Owed You figure on your report.

1. Select the range **E16:G16**.

2. Click the right mouse button to activate a shortcut menu.

3. Select **Border**.

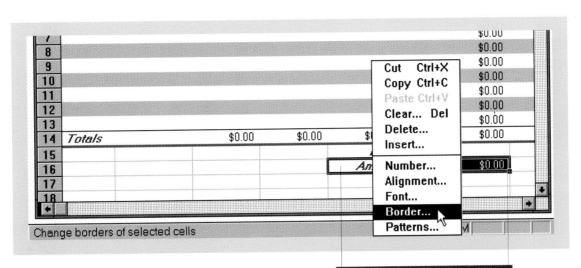

Selected range E16:G16

The Border dialog box will appear.

4. In the dialog box, click **Outline**.

5. Click the **Shade** check box.

6. Click the **Bold Line** option (the top-right selection in the Style area).

7. Click the **Color** drop-down list box.

8. In the drop-down box, click the ↓ scroll button until you see the **Dark Green** color patch, then click that patch.

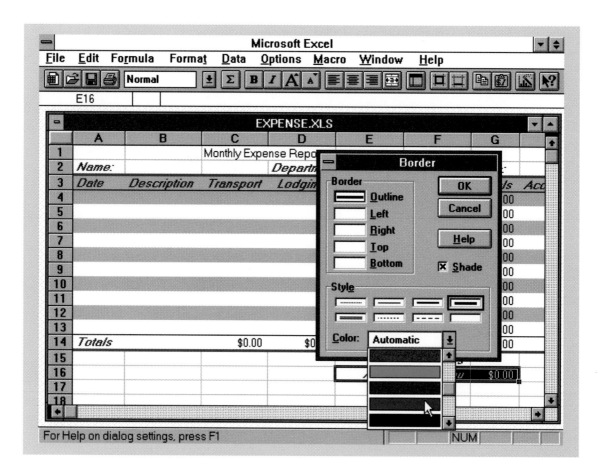

9. Click **OK** to close the dialog box and format the cells.

10. Click any cell *outside* the current selection (E16:G16) to remove the highlight and view the new border and shading.

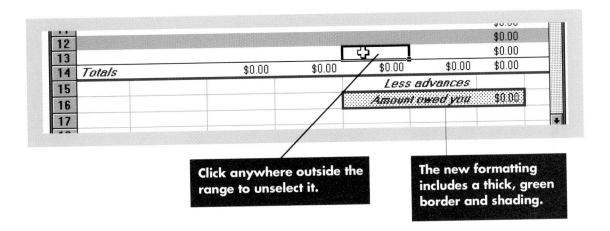

Click anywhere outside the range to unselect it.

The new formatting includes a thick, green border and shading.

Formatting the Sheet Title

You only have to change one more item to complete the formatting of the sheet. Change the font options for the sheet title now, using features in the toolbar.

1. Click cell **C1**.

2. In the toolbar, click the **Bold** tool.

3. Click the **Italic** tool.

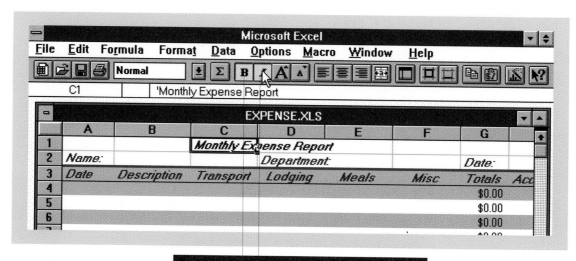

Click the Bold tool, then the Italic tool.

The title should be bigger than the other labels, so fix that now.

4. With cell C1 still selected, click the **Increase Font Size** tool
(to the right of the Italic tool). Watch the change in the size
of the title.

5. Click the **Increase Font Size** tool again. The title will grow
still larger.

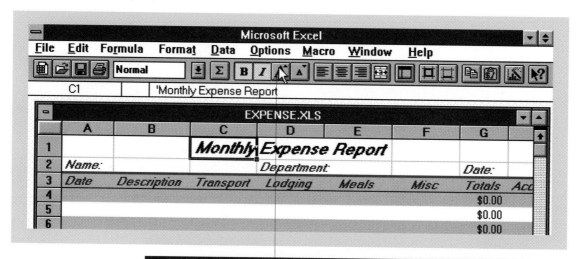

Click the Increase Font Size tool twice (*not* a double click).

Centering the Title

As a final touch, the title should be centered over the form. There is a special tool for this.

1. With cell C1 still selected, move the pointer to the edge of the cell until it changes to an arrow shape, then drag the title label to cell **A1**.

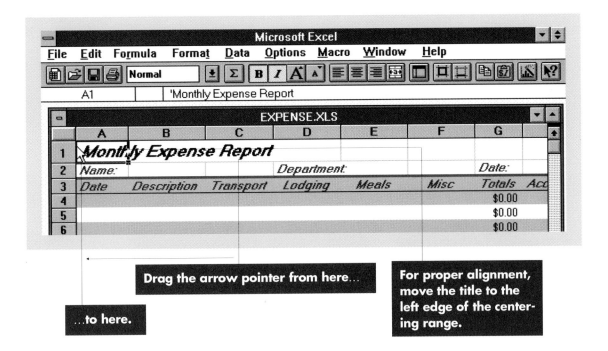

Drag the arrow pointer from here...

...to here.

For proper alignment, move the title to the left edge of the centering range.

2. Select the range **A1:H1**. (Don't be concerned if the sheet display moves, or scrolls.)

3. In the toolbar, click the **Center Across Columns** tool. The title will be centered across the selected range (the entire sheet, in this case).

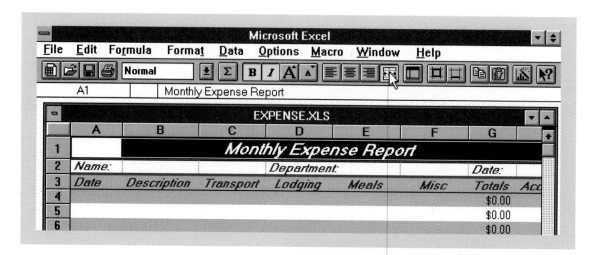

The Center Across Columns tool

Saving the Sheet

You have completed the employee expense report, which is fully functional and self-calculating, as well as attractive in appearance. Save it now to prevent losing all this productive work.

- In the toolbar, click the **Save File** tool (the third icon from the left).

Using the Worksheet

It's time to put the sheet to work for you.

Entering Data

In the following steps, you will enter sample data, as well as learn a new technique for clearing, or erasing, data from the sheet.

1. Select the range **A4:F4**.

2. Type the following data items, pressing ↵ after each entry: **1-2-95**, **Chicago trip**, **465**, **159.23**, **65**, and **15**. The data will appear in the selected range, and the sheet will calculate all required totals. (Note how the program formats the date and currency values automatically.)

2	*Name:*			*Department:*			*Date:*
3	*Date*	*Description*	*Transport*	*Lodging*	*Meals*	*Misc*	*Totals* *Ac*
4	1/2/95	Chicago trip	$465.00	$159.23	$65.00	$15.00	$704.23
5							$0.00
6							$0.00
7							$0.00
8							$0.00
9							$0.00
10							$0.00
11							$0.00
12							$0.00
13							$0.00
14	*Totals*		$465.00	$159.23	$65.00	$15.00	$704.23
15						*Less advances*	

Continue to enter data into the next row, and watch what happens.

3. Select the range **A5:F5**.

4. Type the following data items, pressing ↵ after each entry: **1-7-95**, **Wisconsin tour**, **1293.45**, **487.91**, **589.56**, and **26.00**.

Quick Easy

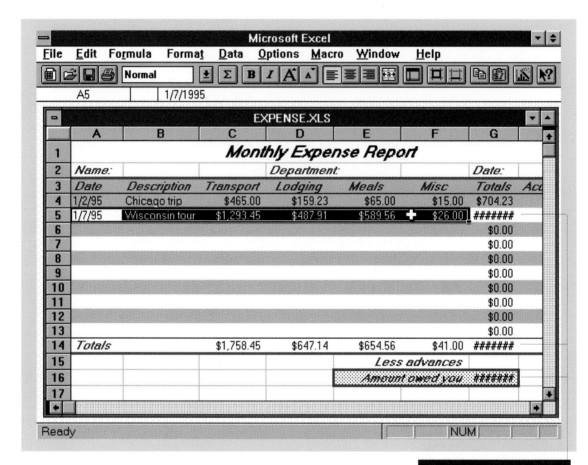

Cell overflow indicator

Adjusting Column Width

Notice the value display in some of the cells. The display shows ####### instead of some of the values. *This is not an error.* It is an indication that the Totals column is not wide enough to hold the calculated values. Fix that now, as you did when you adjusted the width of the Description column.

1. Move the pointer to the right edge of the G column heading so that the pointer changes to a double arrow.

2. Double-click.

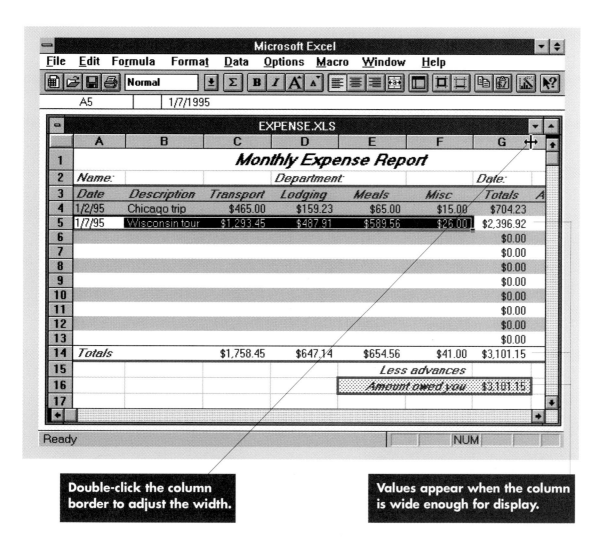

Double-click the column border to adjust the width.

Values appear when the column is wide enough for display.

The program adjusts the column width to fit the longest entry. Values now appear where the overflow indicator (#######) was before.

● Note The sheet includes a column for Account classifications. You will use this column in subsequent lessons.

To save a copy of the current sheet, click the Save File tool.

91

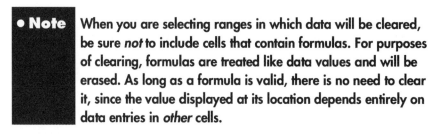

Clearing Data Values

If you want to reuse this sheet, you first have to clear the data values, leaving the formatting intact. Excel 4 provides a convenient way to do this.

1. To select all data values in the sheet, highlight the range **A4:F5**.

> **● Note** When you are selecting ranges in which data will be cleared, be sure *not* to include cells that contain formulas. For purposes of clearing, formulas are treated like data values and will be erased. As long as a formula is valid, there is no need to clear it, since the value displayed at its location depends entirely on data entries in *other* cells.

2. Move the pointer to the fill handle (lower-right corner) of the selected range. The pointer will change to a solid plus sign.

3. Drag the plus sign upward to the top edge of the range, then release the mouse button.

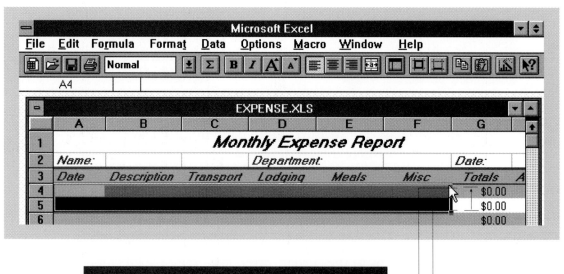

... to here.
To clear data, drag the fill handle from here...

Saving the Sheet as a Template

Clearing all the data values in a sheet is not the most effective way to reuse it. Instead, you can save an empty sheet as a template, or model, for other sheets. If you save the template to the directory XLSTART, the program will present the template in the list of selections whenever you select File ➤ Open. This way, you can create a series of reports without affecting the original sheet.

Save the expense report sheet now as a template.

1. Select **File ➤ Save As**. The Save As dialog box will appear.

2. In the dialog box, open the Save File As Type drop-down list box.

3. From the drop-down list, select **Template**.

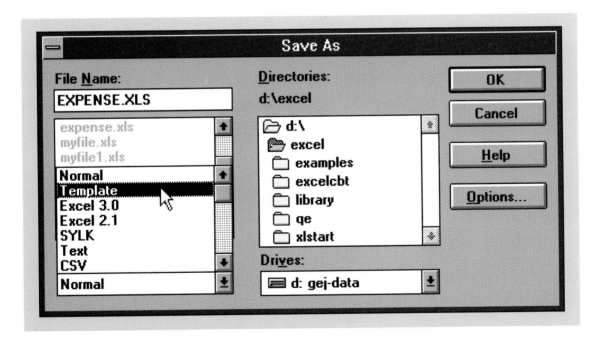

Make a selection now so that the template will become available for automatic start-up.

4. In the Directories list, double-click the **xlstart** subdirectory.

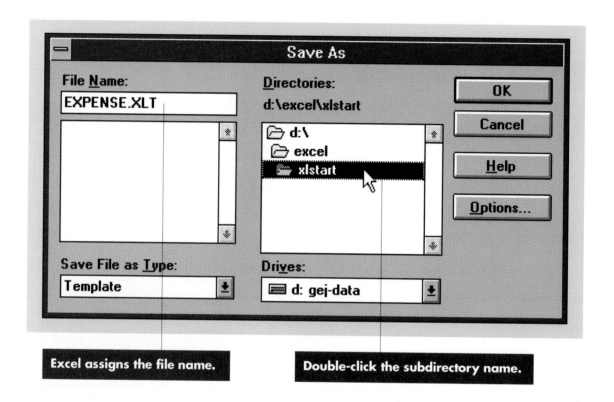

Excel assigns the file name.

Double-click the subdirectory name.

Note that the program automatically picks up the existing file name EXPENSE and appends the file extension for templates, .XLT. Since this name is acceptable, there are no more selections to make in the dialog box.

5. Select **OK** to close the dialog box.

6. Close the sheet file: Select **File ➤ Close**. (You have already saved the sheet in its latest version.)

Applying a Template

Before you end this lesson, you can demonstrate to yourself how using a template can make quick-and-easy work of doing repetitive reports.

1. From the menu bar, select **File ➤ Open**. The Open dialog box will appear.

2. In the File Name list, double-click **expense.xlt**.

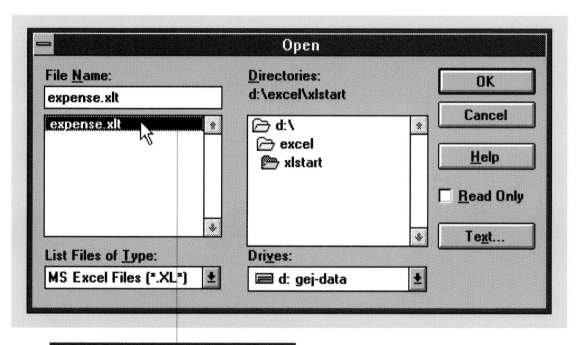

Double-click the template file name.

A new sheet will be opened, formatted according to this template. Note that the program has assigned the name Expense1, which appears in the title bar of the document window.

Quick&Easy

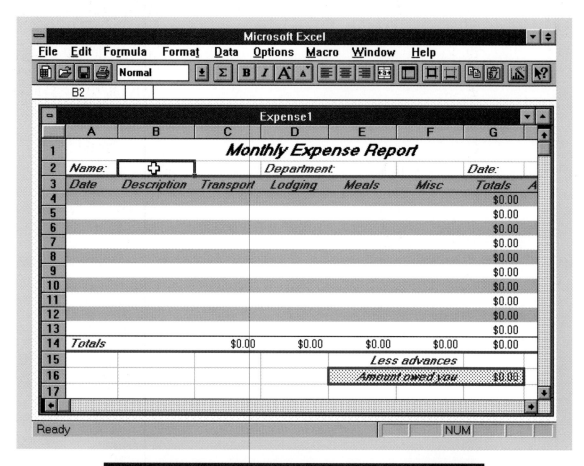

Excel assigns the document title, which will become the file name of this sheet unless you change it when saving.

You can now enter data into this sheet. When you save it, the file name will be EXPENSE1.XLS. The next time you open a sheet by accessing the template, the name Expense2 will be assigned. That is, the program will keep track of the worksheet file names so that they follow one another in sequential order, based on the name of the template from which they were created.

In the next lesson, you will preview and print the expense report.

6 Previewing and Printing the Expense Report

In this lesson, you will be previewing the EXPENSE.XLS sheet on the screen so that you can make final adjustments to its appearance. Then you will print it out as a completed report.

Setting Up Your Printer in Windows

Excel will print only to the default printer, which you must have selected previously in Windows Control Panel. Before continuing this lesson, take the following steps to be sure that your printer is set up properly.

1. If you have the Excel application open, click its **Minimize** button.

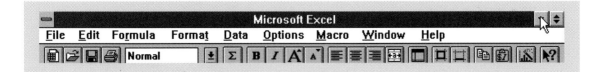

The Excel application will shrink to an icon, and you will be presented with the Program Manager screen.

2. In the Program Manager window, double-click the **Main** program group. The Main group of applications will open.

3. In the Main group, double-click **Control Panel**. The Control Panel window will open.

4. In the Control Panel window, double-click **Printers**. The Printers dialog box will open.

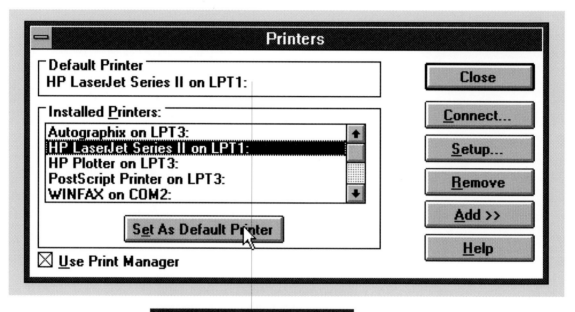

Excel will print to this selection.

If the printer you want to use is not shown here as Default Printer, follow steps 5 and 6.

5. In the Printers dialog box, click the name of the printer you want to use from the Installed Printers list, for example, **HP LaserJet Series II on LPT1:**.

6. In the dialog box, click the button **Set As Default Printer**.

When the correct printer is shown as the default, take the next step.

7. Select **Close** (or **Cancel** if you haven't changed the default printer) to close the Printers dialog box.

Opening the Expense Sheet

Having set up your printer, follow these steps to reopen the sheet you saved at the end of Lesson 5:

1. Restart Excel. (If you minimized it previously, simply double-click its icon in Program Manager.)

2. In the toolbar, click the **Open File** tool. The Open dialog box will appear.

3. In the File Name listing, double-click **expense.xls**. The document window for this file will open.

Making Final Data Entries

To complete the expense report, you will need to enter a few more data items: your name, your department, the date, and the amount of any cash advances.

1. Click cell **B2**.

2. Type *your name* and press ↵.

3. Click cell **E2**.

4. Type **Marketing** and press ↵. (For now, don't be concerned that your entry appears to overwrite the Department label in cell D2.)

5. Click cell **H2**. (Your view of the document will scroll automatically to show column H.)

6. Type **1-31-95** and press ↵.

7. Click cell **G15**.

8. Type **500** and press ↵.

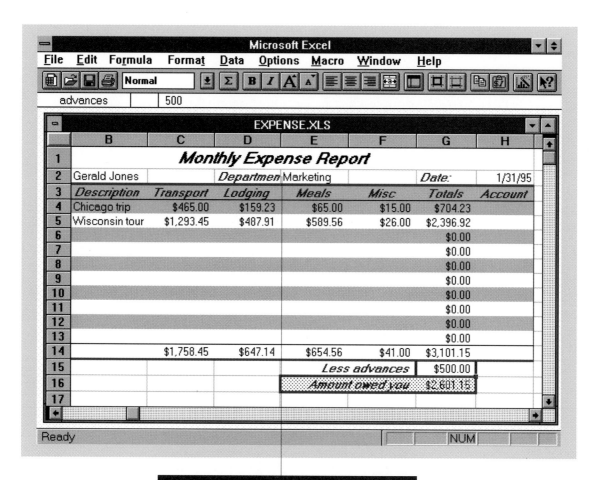

Ignore the overlapping labels (for now).

Previewing the Printed Report

Excel has a way for you to inspect the appearance of the printed document before you produce the actual output. You can also make final adjustments to the appearance of the document at this point.

- While holding down **Shift**, click the **Print** tool, which is located near the left end of the toolbar.

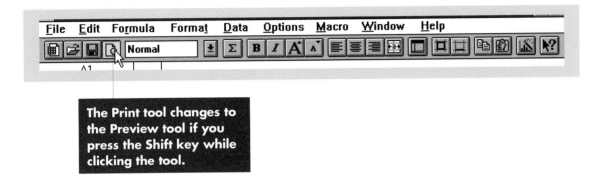

The Print tool changes to the Preview tool if you press the Shift key while clicking the tool.

● **Note** The Print tool icon is a picture of a printer. But when you click this tool while holding down the Shift key, its icon changes to a document symbol with a magnifying glass. This is the Preview tool. This selection is equivalent to choosing File ➤ Print Preview.

A full-screen preview of the sheet will appear.

Changing to Landscape Orientation

In the illustration on the next page, the page is set up initially for portrait orientation, which has the long dimension of the paper running vertically. This is the default printer setting you would want to use if you also do a fair amount of word processing on your computer. However, landscape orientation (in which the long dimension is horizontal) is usually preferred for printing worksheets. You can change this setting within Excel.

1. In the row of buttons at the top of the preview screen, click **Setup**.

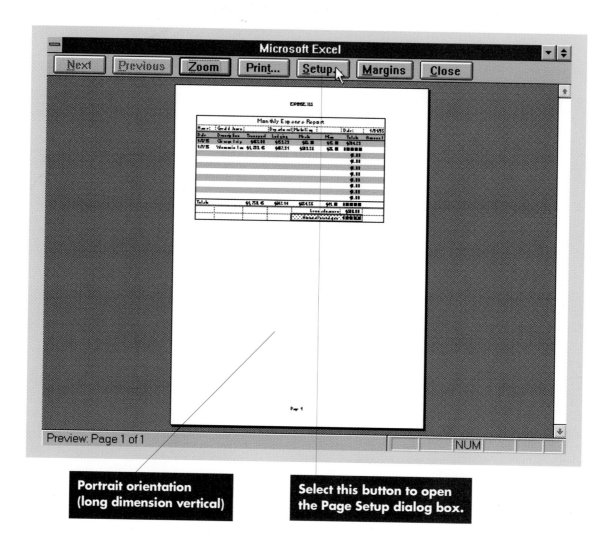

**Portrait orientation
(long dimension vertical)**

**Select this button to open
the Page Setup dialog box.**

The Page Setup dialog box will appear.

2. In the dialog box, click the **Landscape** option button.

3. Be sure that the paper size shown is correct. If not, make
your selection in the Size drop-down list box.

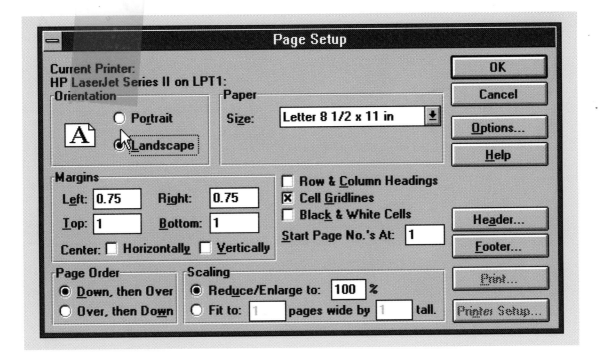

4. Select **OK** to close the dialog box.

Adjusting the Margins

The preview of the sheet will now be shown in landscape orientation. Note that the report is not centered on the page. Fix that now.

- In the row of buttons at the top of the preview screen, click **Margins**.

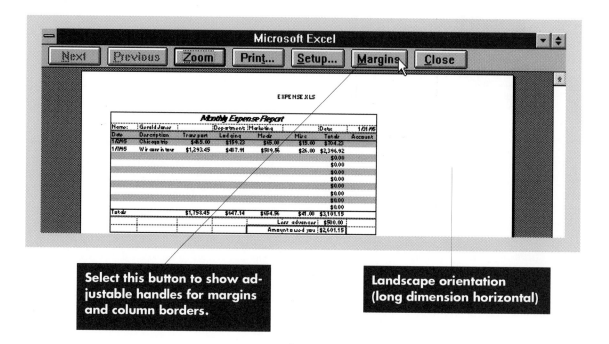

Select this button to show adjustable handles for margins and column borders.

Landscape orientation (long dimension horizontal)

Handles, shown as small black squares, will appear around the edges of the previewed page. The handles at the corners are margins, and the others are column borders. You can adjust any of these—thereby changing the sheet display—simply by dragging the handle. Try this now.

1. Move the pointer to the top leftmost handle on the top edge of the paper (left margin). The pointer will change to a double arrow.

2. Drag the handle to the right to increase the left margin.

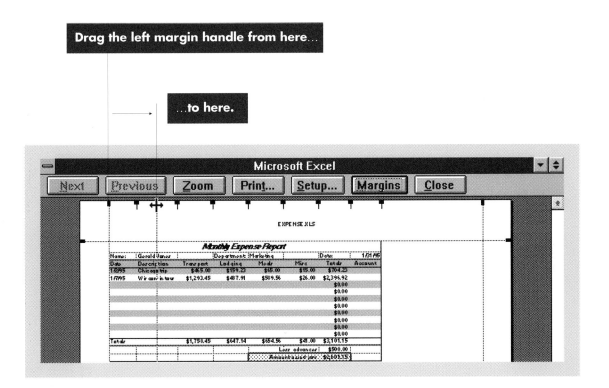

Drag the left margin handle from here...

...to here.

3. Move the pointer to the top handle on the left edge of the paper (top margin). The pointer will change to a double arrow.

4. Drag the handle downward to increase the top margin.

Quick&Easy

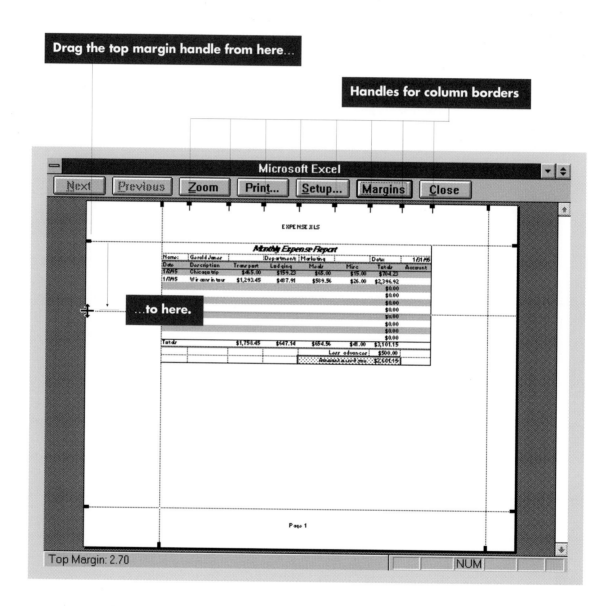

Drag the top margin handle from here...

Handles for column borders

...to here.

● Note If you want to center the report exactly within the margins, there is a quick alternative to dragging the margins in preview mode. In the Page Setup dialog box, select one or both of the Center check boxes: Horizontally and Vertically.

Zooming the View

Recall that the Marketing label you entered appeared to overlap the adjacent Department label. You can inspect this closely without having to print the document first.

1. Move the pointer into the sheet to the Marketing label. The pointer will change to a magnifying glass.

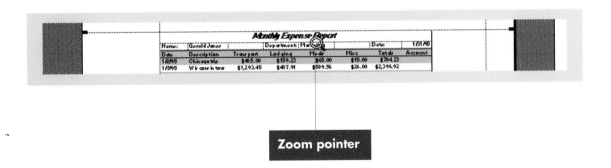

Zoom pointer

2. While the pointer is still shaped like a magnifying glass and positioned over the label, click the left mouse button. A zoomed, or enlarged, view of the sheet will appear.

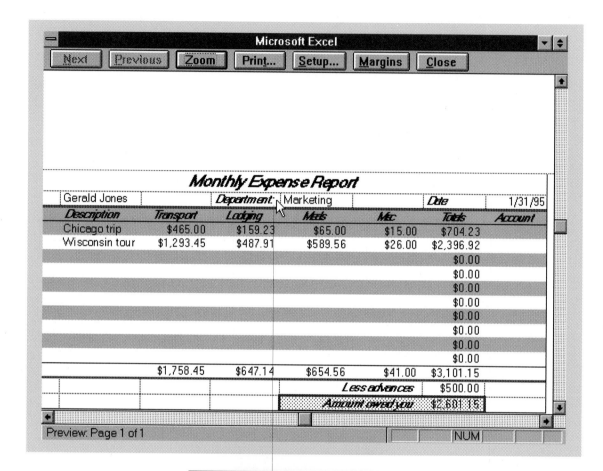

The overlap does not appear.

Unlike the labels in the worksheet window, there is *no* overlap between cells D2 and E2 on the previewed page. That's because the preview is a more precise approximation of the actual printed fonts, spacing, and layout. If there had been an overlap, you could have dragged a margin handle in this preview mode to increase the column width.

Note Zooming the preview will not affect the output itself. It's just a way of inspecting the document more closely. You need not restore the full view before you print, but if you want to do so, click the Zoom button at the top of the screen.

Printing the Sheet

You are now finished with your adjustments to the previewed version of the sheet and can print the document. Be sure that your printer is switched on and the On-Line indicator is lit, then follow these steps:

1. In the row of buttons at the top of the preview screen, click **Print**.

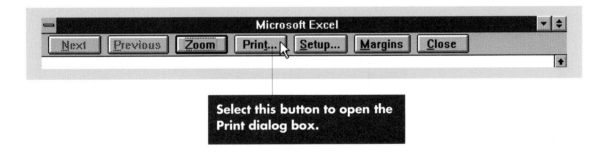

Select this button to open the Print dialog box.

The Print dialog box will appear.

2. If you want multiple copies of the document, type the number in the Copies text box, for example, **2**.

3. Select **OK**.

Quick&Easy

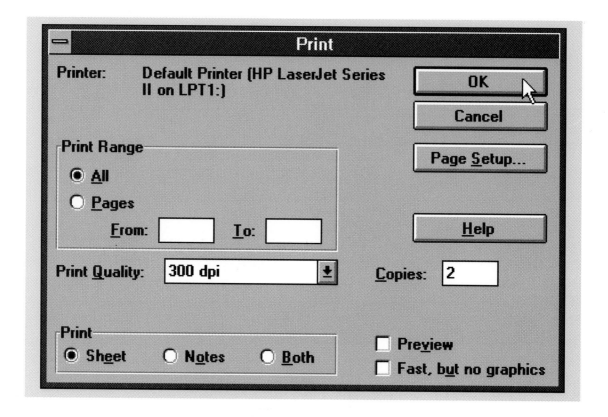

The sheet will print out, and you will return to the worksheet document window. On the printout, note that the program adds the name of the worksheet file at the top of the page and a page number at the bottom.

EXPENSE.XLS

Monthly Expense Report

Name:	Gerald Jones			Department:	Marketing		Date:	1/31/95
Date	Description	Transport	Lodging	Meals	Misc	Totals	Account	
1/2/95	Chicago trip	$465.00	$159.23	$65.00	$15.00	$704.23		
1/7/95	Wisconsin tour	$1,293.45	$487.91	$589.56	$26.00	$2,396.92		
						$0.00		
						$0.00		
						$0.00		
						$0.00		
						$0.00		
						$0.00		
						$0.00		
						$0.00		
Totals		$1,758.45	$647.14	$654.56	$41.00	$3,101.15		
					Less advances	$500.00		
					Amount owed you	$2,601.15		

Matching the Screen to the Output

The printout shown here is from a monochrome laser printer. Colored text on the screen has been converted to black, and colored lines and shading have been reproduced in shades of gray. This conversion is handled not by Excel but by a printer driver program in Windows. For more information about the conversion process, refer to the *Microsoft Windows User's Guide*.

If a font did not print exactly as it appears on the screen, your printer may not be capable of reproducing that font. If you are running Windows version 3.1 or later, you can make the fonts match more closely by following these steps:

1. Save your work and exit Excel.

2. In Program Manager, open the **Main** program group.

3. Select **Control Panel**.

4. Select **Fonts**.

5. The Fonts dialog box will appear. Select the **TrueType** button.

6. The TrueType dialog box will appear. Turn on both check boxes: **Enable TrueType Fonts** and **Show Only TrueType Fonts In Applications**.

7. Select **OK**.

8. In the window that appears, select **Restart Now**. Windows will be restarted automatically, with TrueType fonts enabled.

Using the Print Tool

Setup options, such as printer orientation and page margins, are saved with the Excel sheet, so you only need to set them once, unless you want to change the layout. Once these settings are made, you can print the sheet in a single step.

● When the sheet is open, click the **Print** tool.

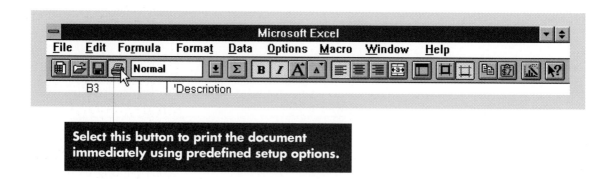

Select this button to print the document immediately using predefined setup options.

The setup options will be bypassed, and the document will be printed immediately.

Printing a Portion of a Sheet

Suppose you only want to print a portion of a sheet. Assuming that setup options have already been selected, you can also do this with the Print tool.

1. In the Expense sheet, select the range **A3:G5**.

2. From the menu bar, select **Options ➤ Set Print Area**.

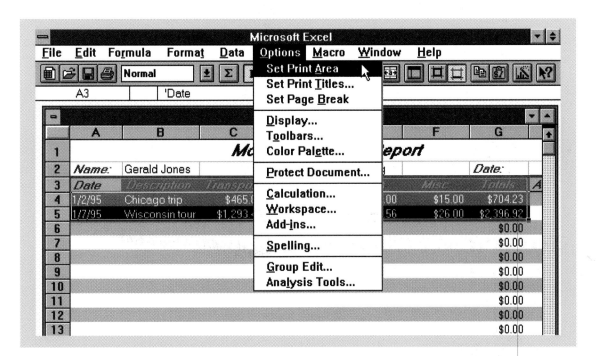

The range A3:G5

3. Click the **Print** tool. Only the selected range will be printed out, using the preselected setup options.

Date	Description	Transport	Lodging	Meals	Misc	Totals
1/2/95	Chicago trip	$465.00	$159.23	$65.00	$15.00	$704.23
1/7/95	Wisconsin tour	$1,293.45	$487.91	$589.56	$26.00	$2,396.92

Saving Your Work

You have completed Lesson 6. Before proceeding to the next lesson, and particularly if you need to quit the program, save your work.

1. With the Expense sheet open, click the **Save File** tool.

2. If you need to quit Excel, select **File ➤ Exit**.

Sorting Expenses by Account

In this lesson, you will apply a feature of Excel 4.0 for Windows that is both quick and easy to use and very powerful—the Sort command. The purpose will be to prepare a breakdown of subtotals for each account, or expense category.

Until now, the Account column of your expense report has been blank. This space is provided for the entry of account numbers to which line items will be charged. The account numbers typically would be taken from your company's chart of accounts, or master list of categories for income and expense items.

In the following steps, you will enter more expense data, assign account numbers to each line of the report, and then sort the data by account number.

Starting Excel and Opening the Sheet

Begin this lesson by starting Excel and opening the Expense sheet. This time, try an alternative way of retrieving the file instead of using the Open File tool.

1. Restart Excel if you have left it.

2. From the menu bar, select **File**. The File pull-down menu will appear.

3. If the Expense sheet is among the last four sheets you worked on, its file name will be listed near the bottom of the pull-down menu. If so, select **EXPENSE.XLS**. (Otherwise, click once *outside* the menu to release it, then click the Open File tool to retrieve the file.)

Entering Expense Data

After you select the file, its document window will open. Now, enter some more expense items into the sheet.

1. Select **A6:F6**.

2. Type the following data entries, pressing ↵ after each one (for <blank> cells, make no entry and just press ↵): **1-10-95**, **Lunch - Apex**, <blank>, <blank>, **54**, **5**.

3. Select **A7:F7**.

4. Type in these entries, pressing ↵ after each one: **1-12-95**, **Dinner - Marcom**, <blank>, <blank>, **184**, **12**.

5. Select **A8:F8**.

6. Enter **1-16-95**, **SIA conference**, **325**, **56**, **23.50**, **3**.

7. Select **A9:F9**.

8. Enter **1-18-95**, **Lunch - XCorp**, <blank>, <blank>, **43**, **2**.

9. Select **A10:F10**.

10. Enter **1-23-95**, **Lunch - Apex**, <blank>, <blank>, **76**, **5**.

11. Select **A11:F11**.

12. Enter **1-25-95**, **Supplies**, <blank>, <blank>, <blank>, **13.93**.

13. Select **A12:F12**.

14. Enter **1-26-95**, **Ohio tour**, **1496.54**, **236**, **154**, **15**.

15. Select **A13:C13**.

16. Enter **1-30-95**, **Car allowance**, **345**.

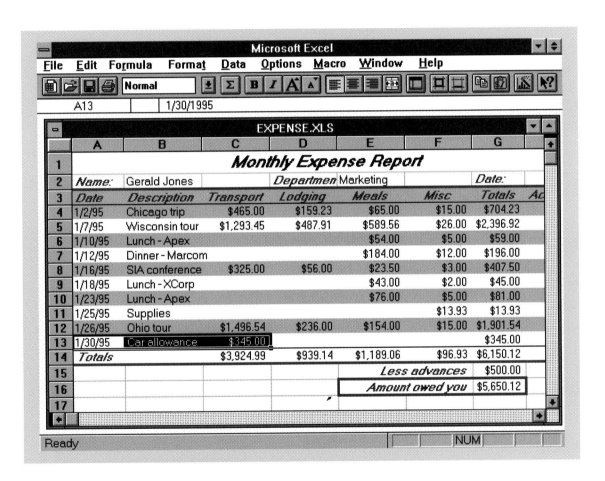

Entering the Account Numbers

You can now assign each of the line items on the report to a specific numbered account. Assume that your company's chart of accounts includes the following categories:

803 Car expense

811 Office expense

816 Travel expense

817 Meals and entertainment

Each of these account numbers, in turn, can have subaccounts, or more specific categories. In the expense report example, there might be a separate subaccount for each client company. For example, Apex Chemicals might be subaccount 17. The account number for meals and entertainment charged to this subaccount, then, would be

817.17

Enter account numbers now for each of the line items in the report.

1. Scroll the display to show column H: Click the **right arrow** button in the horizontal scroll bar.

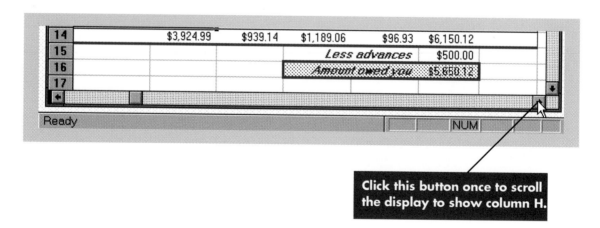

Click this button once to scroll the display to show column H.

2. Select the column **H4:H13**.

3. Type the following entries, pressing ↵ after each one: **816.12, 816.15, 817.17, 817.11, 816.14, 817.18, 817.17, 811, 816.13, 803**.

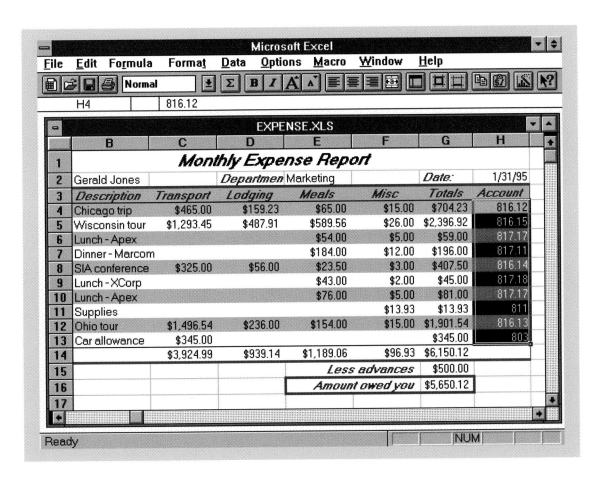

Building a Table

Having entered the account numbers, you should now create a table to hold the sorted account totals.

Selecting the Sort Range

First, you must select the data that will be sorted.

- Select the range **G4:H13**.

It would destroy the chronological order of the report to sort these items in place, or within the report itself. Instead, you should create a separate table.

Copying and Pasting Data Values

To create the table of account totals, you need to copy the selected range to another part of the sheet. However, you don't want to copy the formulas, just the data values. You can do this with the Paste Special command.

1. With the range G4:H13 still highlighted, click the **Copy** tool (the fourth button from the left).

2. Click the **down arrow** button in the vertical scroll bar several times until row 25 is visible.

3. Select the range **B16:C25**.

4. Select **Edit ➤ Paste Special**. The Paste Special dialog box will appear.

5. In the dialog box, select the **Values** option button.

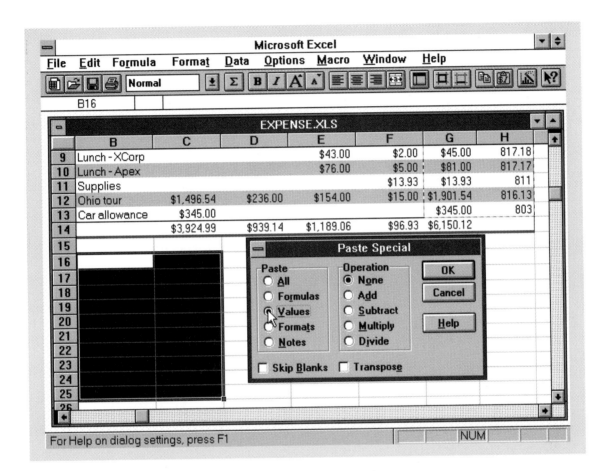

6. Select **OK** to close the dialog box.

The values you copied to the Clipboard will be pasted into the selected range.

Quick&Easy

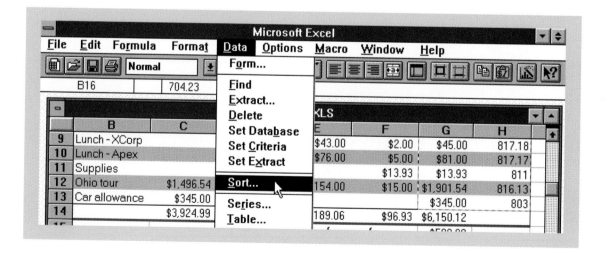

15					*Less advances*	$500.00	
16	704.23	816.12			*Amount owed you*	$5,650.12	
17	2396.92	816.15					
18	59	817.17					
19	196	817.11					
20	407.5	816.14					
21	45	817.18					
22	81	817.17					
23	13.93	811					
24	1901.54	816.13					
25	345	803					
26							

Select destination and press ENTER or choose Paste   NUM

Sorting the Data

You can now sort the data in the table.

1. With the range B16:C25 still highlighted, select **Data ▶ Sort**.

The Sort dialog box will appear with the 1st Key text box already highlighted. You must now type the cell address of the *sort key,* or entry by which the other data will be sorted. In this case, the key will be the account number.

2. Type **c16**.

Type the cell address of the first account number.

3. Select **OK**.

The data in the selected range will now appear in the sheet, sorted by account number in ascending numeric order.

15				*Less advances*	$500.00	
16	345	803		*Amount owed you*	$5,650.12	
17	13.93	811				
18	704.23	816.12				
19	1901.54	816.13				
20	407.5	816.14				
21	2396.92	816.15				
22	196	817.11				
23	59	817.17				
24	81	817.17				
25	45	817.18				
26						

Ready   NUM

Calculating Account Totals

Before you apply appearance formatting to this range, you should calculate totals for each of the accounts.

1. Click cell **D21**.

2. In the toolbar, click the **AutoSum** tool.

3. Drag the pointer to select the range **B18:B21** and press ↵.

4. Click cell **D25**.

5. Click the **AutoSum** tool.

6. Drag the pointer to select the range **B22:B25** and press ↵.

Totals for accounts 816 and 817 will now appear in the selected cells.

	Microsoft Excel						

File Edit Formula Format Data Options Macro Window Help

| Normal | Σ | B | I | A | A | | | | | | |

D25   =SUM(B22:B25)

EXPENSE.XLS

	B	C	D	E	F	G	H
9	Lunch - XCorp			$43.00	$2.00	$45.00	817.18
10	Lunch - Apex			$76.00	$5.00	$81.00	817.17
11	Supplies				$13.93	$13.93	811
12	Ohio tour	$1,496.54	$236.00	$154.00	$15.00	$1,901.54	816.13
13	Car allowance	$345.00				$345.00	803
14		$3,924.99	$939.14	$1,189.06	$96.93	$6,150.12	
15					Less advances	$500.00	
16	345	803			Amount owed you	$5,650.12	
17	13.93	811					
18	704.23	816.12					
19	1901.54	816.13					
20	407.5	816.14					
21	2396.92	816.15	5410.19				
22	196	817.11					
23	59	817.17					
24	81	817.17					
25	45	817.18	381				
26							

Ready   NUM

Formatting the Table

Now you can apply number and appearance formats to the table.

Applying the Currency Format

Perform a multiple selection to which you will apply the Currency number format.

1. Select the range **B16:B25**.

2. While holding down **Ctrl**, click cells **D21** and **D25**.

3. In the toolbar, click the **Style** drop-down list box.

4. From the drop-down list, select **Currency**.

Adding Bottom Borders

A convention in accounting for showing totals is to draw an underscore beneath the values. You can do this in Excel by adding borders to the bottoms of selected cells.

1. Select **B16:C16**.

2. While holding down **Ctrl**, select the following other ranges: **B17:C17, B21:D21, B25:D25**.

3. In the toolbar, click the **Bottom Border** tool (the fifth one from the right).

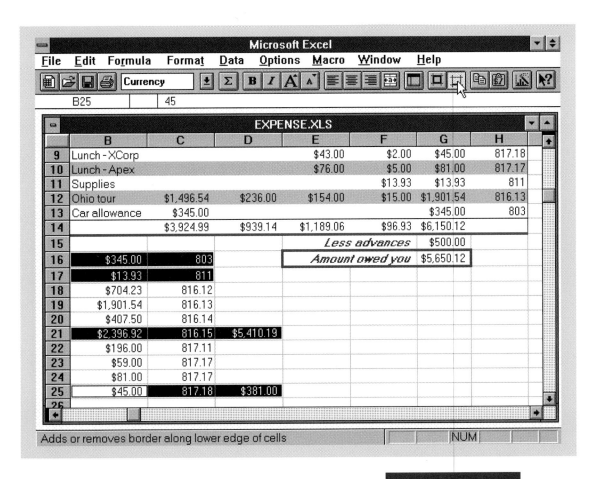

Bottom Border tool

Previewing and Printing the Report

You can now print the revised report. This time, instead of adjusting the margins in preview mode, use a different procedure for centering the report on the page.

1. Select **File ➤ Page Setup**. The Page Setup dialog box will appear.

Quick Easy

2. Check both of the Center boxes: **Horizontally** and **Vertically**.

Page Setup		
Current Printer:		**OK**
HP LaserJet Series II on LPT1:		**Cancel**
Orientation	Paper	**Options...**
○ Portrait Size:	Letter 8 1/2 x 11 in ⬍	**Help**
⊙ Landscape		

Orientation
○ Portrait
⊙ Landscape

Paper
Size: Letter 8 1/2 x 11 in ⬍

Margins
Left: 0.74   Right: 0.75
Top: 0.83   Bottom: 1
Center: ☒ Horizontally ☒ Vertically

☐ Row & Column Headings
☒ Cell Gridlines
☐ Black & White Cells
Start Page No.'s At: 1

Page Order
⊙ Down, then Over
○ Over, then Down

Scaling
⊙ Reduce/Enlarge to: 100 %
○ Fit to: 1 pages wide by 1 tall.

OK
Cancel
Options...
Help
Header...
Footer...
Print...
Printer Setup...

**Select both check boxes
to center the report on
the page.**

3. Select **OK**.

4. In the toolbar, click the **Print** tool. The report will be sent to
the default printer.

EXPENSE.XLS

Monthly Expense Report							
Name:	Gerald Jones		**Department:**	Marketing		**Date:**	1/31/95
Date	**Description**	**Transport**	**Lodging**	**Meals**	**Misc**	**Totals**	**Account**
1/2/95	Chicago trip	$465.00	$159.23	$65.00	$15.00	$704.23	816.12
1/7/95	Wisconsin tour	$1,293.45	$487.91	$589.56	$26.00	$2,396.92	816.15
1/10/95	Lunch - Apex			$54.00	$5.00	$59.00	817.17
1/12/95	Dinner - Marcom			$184.00	$12.00	$196.00	817.11
1/16/95	SIA conference	$325.00	$56.00	$23.50	$3.00	$407.50	816.14
1/18/95	Lunch - XCorp			$43.00	$2.00	$45.00	817.18
1/23/95	Lunch - Apex			$76.00	$5.00	$81.00	817.17
1/25/95	Supplies				$13.93	$13.93	811
1/26/95	Ohio tour	$1,496.54	$236.00	$154.00	$15.00	$1,901.54	816.13
1/30/95	Car allowance	$345.00				$345.00	803
Totals		$3,924.99	$939.14	$1,189.06	$96.93	$6,150.12	
					Less advances	$500.00	
	$345.00	803			**Amount owed you**	$5,650.12	
	$13.93	811					
	$704.23	816.12					
	$1,901.54	816.13					
	$407.50	816.14					
	$2,396.92	816.15	$5,410.19				
	$196.00	817.11					
	$59.00	817.17					
	$81.00	817.17					
	$45.00	817.18	$381.00				

The expense report now includes a table of charges by account number, with totals for each account.

Saving Your Work

You have completed Lesson 7. Before proceeding to the next lesson, and particularly if you need to quit the program, save your work.

Creating a Worksheet Outline

The expense report that you have built up in previous lessons is a summary of expenditures for a month of business activities. Even though you show only summary totals in the report, you would normally be expected to keep detailed records to back up those totals. It would be convenient, then, to include the supporting information in the worksheet file, yet be able to suppress it when the sheet is printed.

This is just one application of the Formula ➤ Outline command in Excel 4. In this lesson, you will add expense subtotals to the Expense sheet, then provide a way for displaying them selectively by outlining the sheet. You will also learn how to include text comments and notes in your worksheets.

Starting Excel and Opening the Sheet

Begin this lesson by starting Excel and opening the EXPENSE.XLS sheet. Use the Open File tool. If you need help, refer to the procedure at the beginning of Lesson 7.

Inserting New Rows in the Sheet

In its present form, there is no place in the sheet for itemized expenses. Provide for these entries now by inserting two more rows within the existing sheet.

1. Click cell **B5**.

2. Select **Edit ➤ Insert.** The Insert dialog box will appear.

3. In the dialog box, select **Entire Row.**

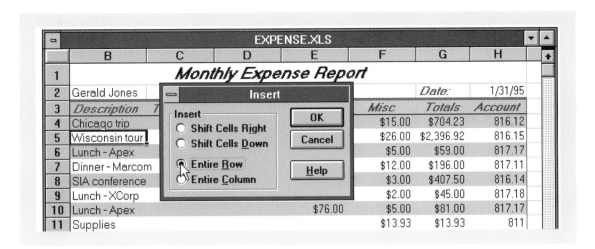

4. Select **OK.** A new row will appear in the sheet above the cell you selected. The current cell is still B5, but it is now the first cell in the new row.

5. With B5 still selected, repeat steps 2–4 to add another row to the sheet.

Itemizing Your Expenses

You now have two empty rows beneath the row of expense items for the Chicago trip. You can use these rows to hold an itemization of your expenses.

1. Select the range **B5:C6.**

2. Type the following data entries, pressing ⏎ after each one: **Air fare, Car rental, 342, 123.**

	B	C	D	E	F	G	H
		EXPENSE.XLS					
1		*Monthly Expense Report*					
2	Gerald Jones		*Departmen*	Marketing		*Date:*	1/31/95
3	*Description*	*Transport*	*Lodging*	*Meals*	*Misc*	*Totals*	*Account*
4	Chicago trip	$465.00	$159.23	$65.00	$15.00	$704.23	816.12
5	Air fare	$342.00					
6	Car rental	$123.00					
7	Wisconsin tour	$1,293.45	$487.91	$589.56	$26.00	$2,396.92	816.15
8	Lunch - Apex			$54.00	$5.00	$59.00	817.17
9	Dinner - Marcom			$184.00	$12.00	$196.00	817.11
10	SIA conference	$325.00	$56.00	$23.50	$3.00	$407.50	816.14
11	Lunch - XCorp			$43.00	$2.00	$45.00	817.18

Updating Formulas in the Sheet

For the sheet to be set up properly for outlining, the amount in cell C4 must actually be a summary of the new items you've entered. Provide for that now by using the AutoSum tool.

1. Click cell **C4**.

2. In the toolbar, click the **AutoSum** tool.

3. Drag the pointer so that the moving dotted line surrounds **C5:C6**.

4. Press ↵.

Cell C4 now holds the formula =SUM(C5:C6) so that its entry is a summary of the itemized expenses.

However, the sheet as it is currently built will produce incorrect results. Note that your new data entries have been erroneously included in the total figure in cell C16. To exclude the subtotals, you must redefine the range called Transport.

5. With cell **C4** still selected, hold down Ctrl while you drag the pointer to select the range C7:C15.

6. Select **Formula ➤ Define Name**. The Define Name dialog box will appear.

7. In the Name text box, type **Transport**.

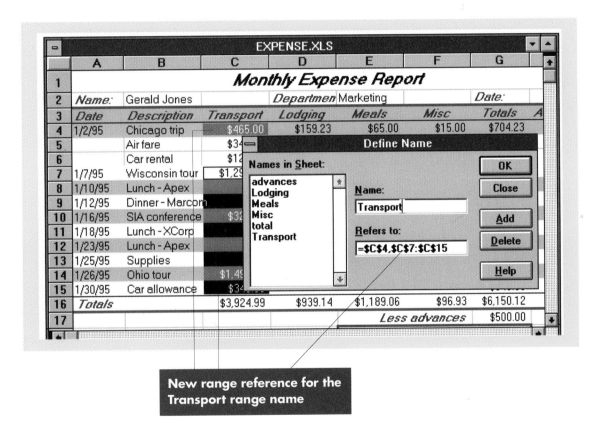

New range reference for the Transport range name

8. Select **OK**.

The Transport range name has been redefined to contain the cell C4 and the range C7:C15, excluding the amounts in C5 and C6.

> **● Note** These detailed expense entries are shown here to illustrate the Outline feature of Excel 4. If you actually use this sheet and insert other itemized expenses, you will have to update any range names or formulas that might otherwise include them. That is, if you insert more rows and itemized expenses in the Transport, Lodging, Meals, and Misc ranges, you will have to redefine those range names so that the formulas in row 16 will generate correct column totals.

Creating an Outline

A worksheet outline makes selected rows or columns (or both) subordinate to other rows or columns in a sheet. The result is that the subordinate entries can be alternately displayed or hidden on command. Follow these steps to see how this works:

1. Select the range A3:G6.

2. Select Formula ➤ Outline. The Outline dialog box will appear.

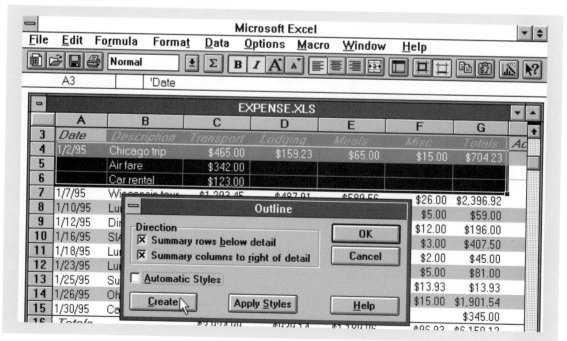

3. In the dialog box, select **Create**.

The display changes to include buttons for manipulating the sheet as a multiple-level outline.

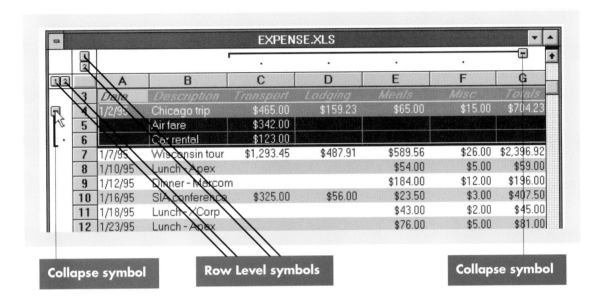

Collapse symbol **Row Level symbols** **Collapse symbol**

Controlling the Outline Display

At the left edge of the sheet will appear Row Level symbols labeled 1 and 2, as well as a Collapse symbol, which is labeled with a minus sign (–). These symbols are buttons that you can click to control the display of the outline.

Hiding the Subordinate Rows

You can hide the subordinate rows, or collapse the outline, literally at the touch of a button. Try it now.

- Click the **Collapse** button.

Quick Easy

The subordinate rows will be hidden, and the Collapse button will turn into an Expand button, labeled with a plus sign (+).

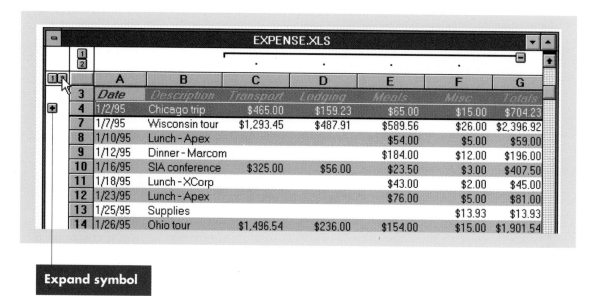

Expand symbol

Revealing the Subordinate Rows

You can simply click the Expand button to restore the outline to its expanded form, revealing the subordinate rows. As an alternative—especially if an outline includes multiple levels—you can click the Row Level symbol of the view you want. In this case, the outline has two levels. Restore the original view of the sheet now.

● Click the Row Level symbol labeled **2**.

The expanded sheet will reappear.

> **● Note** Depending on the layout of a sheet, you may also see buttons at the top of the window for collapsing/expanding the columns. You can control the printing of subordinate rows or columns the same way you control the display. Outlines are WYSIWYG (What You See Is What You Get): The printout will match the screen display.

Annotating the Sheet with Text

You might also want to add text comments or notes in a worksheet. There are two kinds of annotations: text boxes that are printed with the document, and text notes that are included in the file but normally hidden from view.

Adding a Text Box

A text box is an annotation to a sheet that will normally be printed out. However, because you have created an outline in this sheet, you can add a reminder to yourself among the subordinate entries. This text box will therefore be printed only if you print the outline in its expanded form.

1. Move the pointer to any position in the toolbar, and click the right mouse button. A shortcut menu will appear.

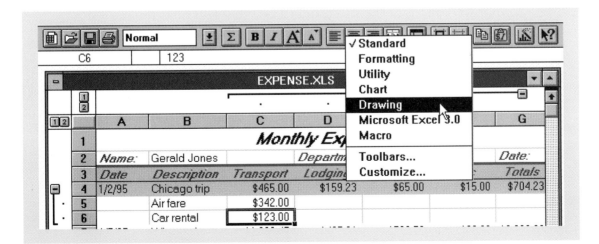

Quick&Easy

2. From the shortcut menu, select **Drawing**. The Drawing tool-bar will appear.

Text Box tool

● **Note** The Drawing toolbar can also appear at any edge of the display. You can drag any of the toolbars to any position on the screen. If you move a toolbar within a sheet window, it will appear (as shown here) in its own window—with its own title bar and Control box. You can resize such a toolbar window by dragging any of its borders.

3. In the toolbar, click the **Text Box** tool.

4. In rows 5 and 6 of the sheet, drag a box that will hold the text. When you release the mouse button, a flashing I-beam cursor will appear inside the box.

5. Type **Cash for gas: $14.95.**

6. Click anywhere outside the text box.

**Click the Control box
to close the toolbar.**

7. To close the Drawing toolbar, click its Control box (in the
top-left corner).

Adding a Note

Unlike a text box, a note is a text annotation that will not be printed
with the sheet. Add a note now that will help document the way you
built this sheet.

1. Click cell **A5**.

2. Select **Formula ➤ Note**. The Cell Note dialog box will appear.

3. In the Text Note box, type

If subordinate rows are added, be sure to update all affected range
names and formulas!

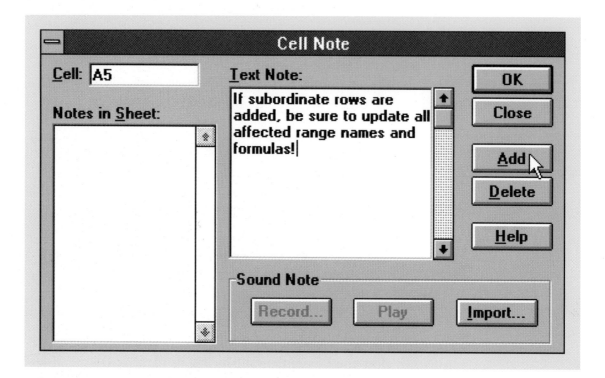

4. In the dialog box, select **Add**.

5. Select **OK** to close the dialog box.

A small red dot will appear in the top-right corner of the cell that contains the note. The dot will not be shown when the sheet is previewed or printed.

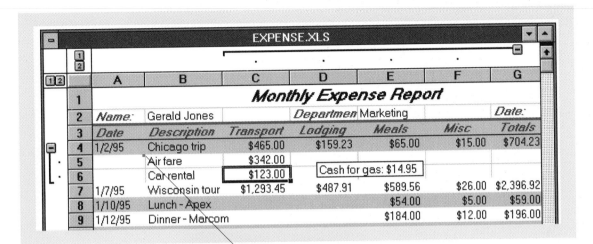

The red dot indicates that the cell contains a note.

● Note   A worksheet can contain many notes, one in each cell. To view notes after you have added them to a sheet, select Formula ➤ Note, then click the cell in the Notes In Sheet list box. When you are finished reading the notes, select the Close button. The note indicator will appear only when the Note Indicator option is checked in Options ➤ Workspace.

Saving Your Work

All the features you have added to the Expense sheet—the outline, text box, and note—will be saved in the worksheet file and will be available whenever you reopen it. Before you exit Excel and while the Expense sheet is open and active, save the file.

10 MINUTES

Linking Worksheets in a Workbook

9

There will be times when you want to transfer results from one worksheet to another. It would be most convenient if you could have the program do this for you, without your having to reenter the data. With Excel for Windows, you can link worksheets to share data. Updates will be automatic, so a change in one sheet will affect all the others to which it is linked. (You can also share data among Windows applications, but that topic is beyond the scope of this book.)

In accounting, for example, the need for data links arises when you must carry the results of a supporting schedule to a ledger. In the expense report, it will be necessary to carry the expense totals from individual expense reports to a management-level report that summarizes expenses for the department. In this lesson, you will build a portion of the departmental sheet, then link it to your own expense sheet. Then, to make it easy to access both sheets, you will consolidate them in a single disk file called a *workbook*.

Starting Excel and Opening the Sheet

Begin this lesson by starting Excel and opening the Expense sheet. Use the Open File tool. If you need help, refer to the procedure at the beginning of Lesson 7.

Building the Departmental Summary

You can have several sheets open at the same time in Excel 4 for Windows. When the program starts, it opens an empty sheet, which it titles

Sheet1. When you open the Expense sheet, the first sheet becomes inactive but remains open.

Arranging the Document Windows

Follow these steps to display and work on both sheets at the same time:

1. Select **Window ➤ Arrange**. The Arrange Windows dialog box will appear.

2. From the Arrange options, select **Horizontal**.

3. Select **OK**.

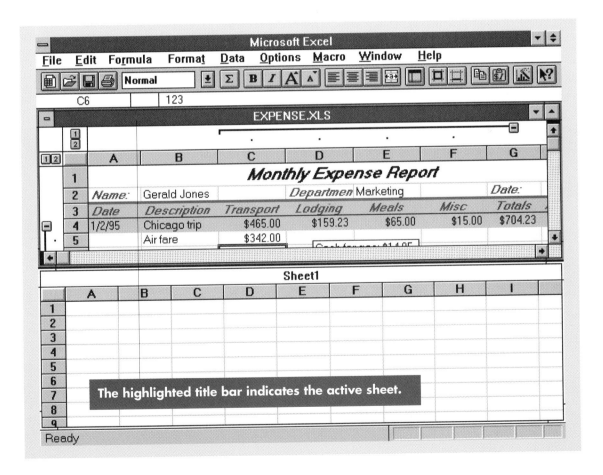

The highlighted title bar indicates the active sheet.

Note that the title bar of the Expense sheet is highlighted, indicating that its window is active. Only one window, the one you are working in, can be active at a time. Activate the Sheet1 window.

4. Click the title bar of Sheet1.

Its title bar is now highlighted, indicating that the sheet is active.

Entering Column Headings

Begin to build the new sheet by entering its column labels.

1. Select the range **A2:C2**.

2. Type **Employee, Date, Expenses** (pressing ↵ after each entry).

3. Click the **Center Align** tool.

	A	B	C	D	E	F	G	H	I
1									
2	Name	Date	Expenses						
3									
4									

Sheet1

Creating a Data Link

All of the data you need to show in Sheet1 from your own expense report are already contained in the Expense sheet.

Using the Paste Link Command

Transfer a data item now, creating a link in the process.

1. In the Expense sheet, click cell **B2** twice. (The sheet window will be activated automatically the first time you click any of its cells.)

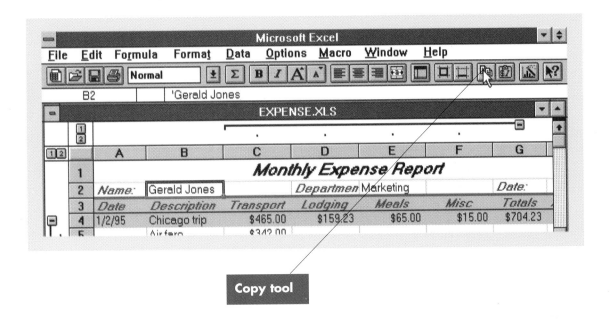

Copy tool

2. In the toolbar, click the **Copy** tool (the fourth icon from the right).

A moving dotted line will surround the selected cell, indicating that its contents have been copied to the Windows Clipboard. Now, paste the data into the other sheet.

3. Move the pointer into the Sheet1 window and click cell **A4** twice.

4. Select **Edit ➤ Paste Link**.

Quick Easy

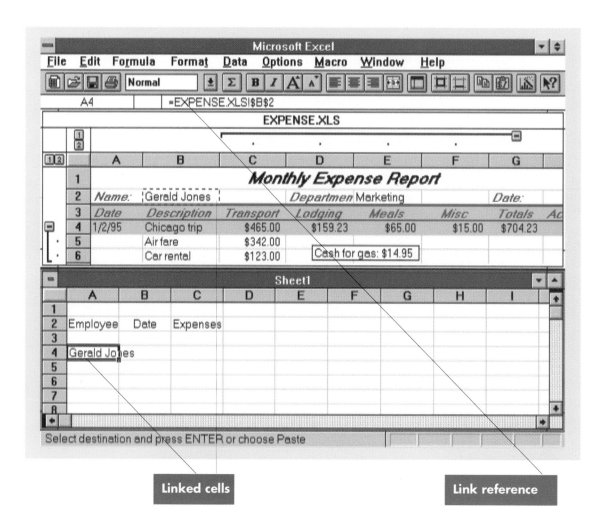

Linked cells

Link reference

Verifying the Data Link

The data from the Clipboard will appear in the selected cell of Sheet1.
When this cell is selected, note the entry in the formula bar:

=EXPENSE.XLS!B2

This reference indicates the source of the linked data. The formula symbol, the equal sign (=), is followed by the file name (EXPENSE), including its extension (.XLS). Next come an exclamation point (!) and the address of the cell that holds the data (B2). The dollar signs indicate that the address won't change.

> **• Note** If you do not see a link reference in the formula bar after you perform the Paste Link command, a link was not established. You should check to be sure that you are requesting a valid link, then redo the command.

Creating Other Links

There can be multiple links between sheets, so you can let the program do the work of entering the rest of the required items from your report.

1. Click the title bar of EXPENSE.XLS to activate the sheet. A set of scroll bars will appear.

2. Adjust the horizontal scroll bar by clicking its **right arrow** button until cell H2 is visible.

3. Click cell **H2**.

4. Click the **Copy** tool. A moving dotted line will appear around the selected cell.

Quick & Easy

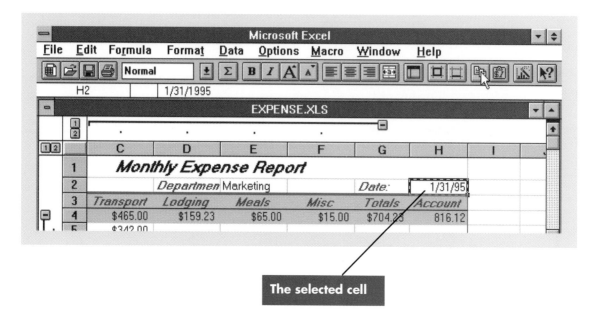

The selected cell

5. Move the pointer into the Sheet1 window and click cell **B4**
twice.

6. Select **Edit ➤ Paste Link**.

7. Repeat steps 1–6, this time adjusting the vertical scroll bar
until cell **G16** is visible, then copy and paste its contents
with a link into cell **C4** of Sheet1.

8. Adjust the display of Sheet1 to increase the width of column
A: Double-click on the right border of the column heading.

9. With cell C4 still selected, click the Style drop-down box,
then select **Currency**.

C4	=EXPENSE.XLS!total

EXPENSE.XLS

	B	C	D	E	F	G	H
12	Lunch - Apex			$76.00	$5.00	$81.00	817.17
13	Supplies				$13.93	$13.93	811
14	Ohio tour	$1,496.54	$236.00	$154.00	$15.00	$1,901.54	816.13
15	Car allowance	$345.00				$345.00	803
16		$3,924.99	$939.14	$1,189.06	$96.93	$6,150.12	
17					*Less advances*	$500.00	
18	$345.00	803			*Amount owed you*	$5,650.12	

Sheet1

	A	B	C	D	E	F	G	H	I
1									
2	Employee	Date	Expenses						
3									
4	Gerald Jones	1/31/95	$6,150.12						
5									
6									
7									

Linked cells

Using Linked Worksheets

You now have all the data you need from your expense report, which is linked to the management summary.

Making Updates

If you make a change in the Expense sheet that affects any of the linked cells, the linked entry in Sheet1 will be updated also.

1. Move the pointer into the Expense sheet and click cell **C15**.

2. Type **350** and press ↵.

13	Supplies				$13.93	$13.93	811
14	Ohio tour	$1,496.54	$236.00	$154.00	$15.00	$1,901.54	816.13
15	Car allowance	$350.00				$350.00	803
16		$3,929.99	$939.14	$1,189.06	$96.93	$6,155.12	
17					*Less advances*	$500.00	

	A	B	C	D	E	F	G	H	I
1									
2	Employee	Date	Expenses						
3									
4	Gerald Jones	1/31/95	$6,155.12						
5									
6									

Sheet1

An update here...

...triggers updates here.

Because you changed the data item in cell C15, the totals in cells C16, G16, and G18 changed in the Expense sheet, according to the formulas in each of those cells. Note that the amount shown in cell C4 of Sheet1 also changed, since it is linked to the corresponding total in the other sheet.

Linking Other Sheets

You could open further sheets, such as the expense reports of other employees, and link them to the management summary just as you did here to create a report for a whole department.

Saving the Sheets in a Workbook

Excel for Windows provides a special type of file, the workbook, in which you can store multiple sheets that are related to one another. This is particularly handy in situations such as this expense report example, in which you always work on the same set of sheets as a group.

> **● Note** Consolidating sheets in workbooks is not necessary for their data links to be maintained. If you open a file that contains a link to another file that is closed, the program will ask you whether the link should be updated: "Update references to unopened documents? (Yes or No)."

1. With sheets Expense and Sheet1 both open, select File ➤ Save Workbook.

A workbook document window, as well as the Save As dialog box, will appear.

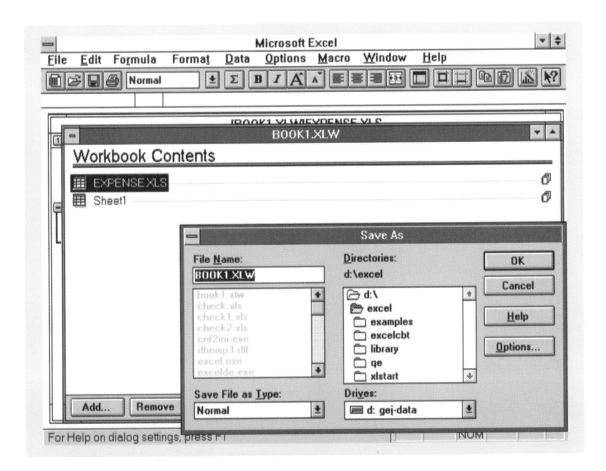

2. In the Save As dialog box, optionally type a file name (or use the default name BOOK1.XLW already shown), and select **OK**.

When you use File ➤ Open or the Open File tool to open a workbook instead of an individual sheet, the workbook document window shown above will appear. You can double-click any of the sheet names listed to open the sheet.

When a sheet is contained in a workbook, a special set of buttons will appear in the bottom-right corner of its document window.

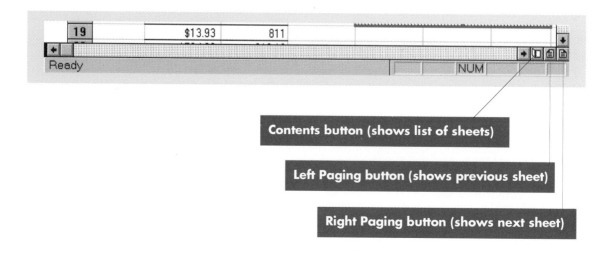

Contents button (shows list of sheets)

Left Paging button (shows previous sheet)

Right Paging button (shows next sheet)

Click the Contents button to reopen the workbook document window, with its list of sheets. Or click the Right Paging button or Left Paging button to move to the previous or next sheet in the workbook.

• Note In this example, Sheet1 was not saved as a separate file and can be accessed only by opening the Book1 workbook. However, you could also use the File ➤ Save command or Save File tool to save Sheet1 as a separate file. If you do this and want to be able to work on the file by itself, select its name in the workbook document window, then select the Options button at the bottom. The Document Options dialog box will appear. Select Separate File, then OK.

Charting and Production Shortcuts

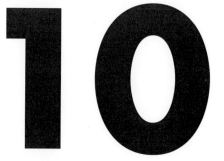

If you have worked through the lessons to this point, you already know how to build and format a fully functional worksheet, and how to print it out. In short, you have all the skills you need to get useful results from Excel for Windows. Beyond the basics, however, the program includes a wealth of other powerful tools, which are just too numerous to include in this short book.

For example, you can connect to external databases, build data tables in Excel, and perform cross-tabulation. The program can consolidate unlike worksheets to form summary sheets automatically. And you can construct what-if scenarios to test different assumptions about a problem.

This final lesson will serve as an introduction to this wider world of Excel. You will work with two of the program's most popular enhancements: the ChartWizard and Check Spelling tools. In using these features, you will also discover some further uses of AutoFill.

Starting Excel and Opening the Sheet

Begin this lesson by starting Excel. There is no need to open a file. You will be working in the default document window Sheet1, which should open automatically when you start the program.

Building a Sheet for Charting

Just about any worksheet you create can be charted, but the real question becomes: What makes a meaningful chart? Ideally, a chart should highlight relationships in the data that might be difficult to see in the tabular form of a worksheet.

In the following steps, you will build a table that breaks down the hours you might spend doing specific tasks in a typical workweek. Charting these data should highlight the tasks that might be taking up too much of your time.

Entering Labels

Begin to build the sheet by entering its title, column headings, and row labels.

1. Click cell **A1**.

2. Type **Productivity Study** and press ↵.

3. Select the range **A1:F1**.

4. Click the **Center Across Columns** tool (the eighth icon from the right in the toolbar).

5. Select the range **B2:F2**.

6. Type the following entries, pressing ↵ after each: **Phone, Mail, Filing, Meetings, Other**.

7. Click the **Center Align** tool.

8. Click cell **A3**.

9. Type **Mon** and press ↵.

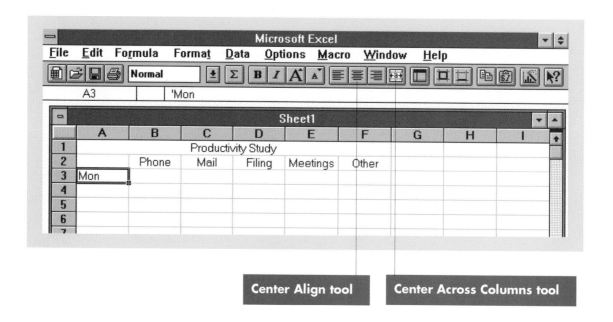

Center Align tool　　**Center Across Columns tool**

You have entered an abbreviation for Monday in cell A3. Now use a
handy feature of AutoFill to generate the rest of the days of the week
automatically.

10. With cell A3 still selected, move the pointer to the fill handle (in the bottom-right corner of the cell highlight). The pointer will change to a solid plus sign.

11. Drag the plus sign from **A3** to **A7** and release the mouse button.

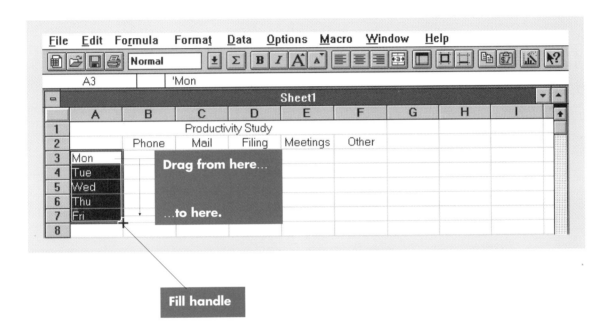

Remember this handy feature of AutoFill! Dragging the fill handle when the first cell contains calendar data will generate a sequence of values instead of merely copying the item.

> **• Note** In some cases, it will be necessary to provide the first two items in the series. If you do this with specific dates, even end-of-month dates will be generated properly. For example, if you enter 2/28/95 and 3/31/95, the program will correctly set the next item to 4/30/95.

Entering the Data

You can use this same feature of AutoFill to generate estimates and projections. Try this now to estimate the number of hours spent on the phone.

1. Select the range **B3:B4**.

2. Type **2.6** and **2.2**, pressing ↵ after each.

3. With the range still selected, move the pointer to the fill handle and drag it to **B7**.

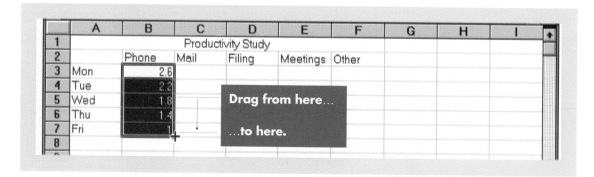

Notice what happened. The second data item you entered differs from the first by 0.4. When you used AutoFill, the program lowered the value of each of the following items in the series by this amount.

This automatic projection feature of AutoFill works best when the series of data items follows a *linear trend* (that is, when it increases or decreases steadily). However, your work patterns probably don't follow such convenient trends. Enter the rest of the actual data in the sheet now, overwriting the linear projections.

4. Select the range **B5:B7**.

5. Type **2.1**, **2.8**, and **2.4**, pressing ↵ after each.

6. Select the range **C3:F7**.

7. Type the following entries, pressing ↵ after each: **1.2, 0.8, 1.3, 1.5, 2.1, 0.4, 0.6, 0.8, 0.7, 1, 2.5, 3, 2.4, 2, 2.2, 1.4, 1.6, 1.4, 0.6, 0.4**.

	A	B	C	D	E	F	G	H	I
1			Productivity Study						
2		Phone	Mail	Filing	Meetings	Other			
3	Mon	2.6	1.2	0.4	2.5	1.4			
4	Tue	2.2	0.8	0.6	3	1.6			
5	Wed	2.1	1.3	0.8	2.4	1.4			
6	Thu	2.8	1.5	0.7	2	0.6			
7	Fri	2.4	2.1	1	2.2	0.4			

Formatting the Sheet

Now that you've built the sheet, you might as well take a quick-and-easy step to make it more attractive.

1. Select the range **A1:F7**.

2. Click the **AutoFormat** tool (the seventh icon from the right in the toolbar).

3. Click outside the range to release the selection and view the sheet in its new colors.

> **• Note** The AutoFormat tool will apply the last format you used. In this case, the format applied is Classic 3. Yours might be different.

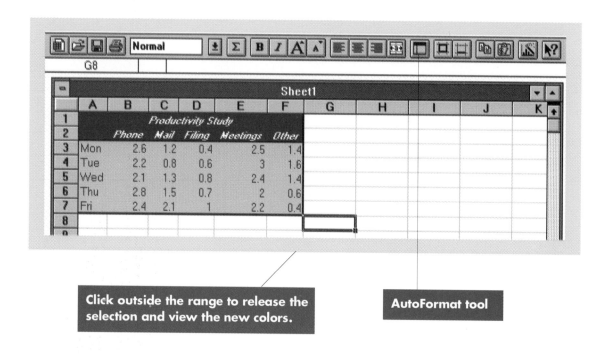

Click outside the range to release the selection and view the new colors.

AutoFormat tool

Saving the Sheet

Before you go any further, it would be a good idea to save the sheet to disk. This way, even if you make an error later, you can always select File ➤ Close, abandon the erroneous changes, and reopen a completed worksheet.

1. In the toolbar, select the **Save File** tool (the third icon from the left).

2. Type **time** and select **OK**.

The sheet will be saved to disk in the file TIME.XLS.

Generating a Chart

Excel 4 for Windows provides the ChartWizard tool for generating charts. Try it now to plot the data from the productivity study.

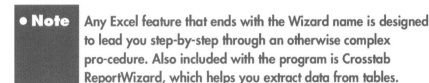

Note Any Excel feature that ends with the Wizard name is designed to lead you step-by-step through an otherwise complex pro-cedure. Also included with the program is Crosstab ReportWizard, which helps you extract data from tables.

1. Select the range **A2:F7** (the whole sheet *except* its title).

Quick&Easy

2. Click the **ChartWizard** tool (the second icon from the right
in the toolbar). A moving dotted line will appear around the
selected range, and the pointer will change to cross hairs.

You must draw an area that will hold the chart.

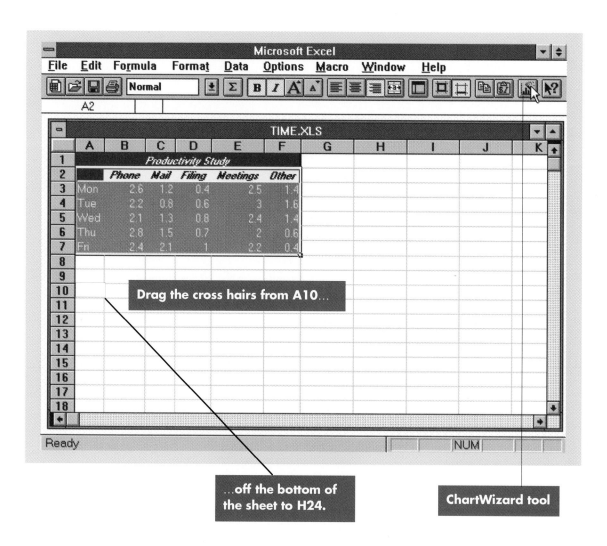

3. Drag the pointer from **A10** to **H24**. (The display will scroll as you move the pointer downward and to the right to select the second corner.)

The first of five dialog boxes will appear: ChartWizard - Step 1 of 5. The range reference for the area you drew appears in its text box.

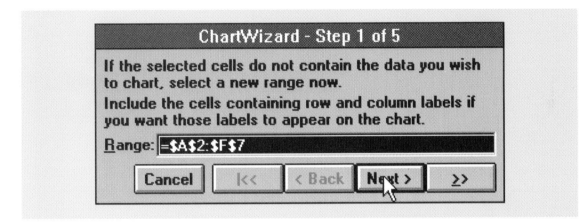

4. In the Step 1 dialog box, select **Next** to accept the range shown and advance to the next step.

The Step 2 dialog box will appear, showing a variety of chart types. You will use the default setting, Column.

Quick Easy

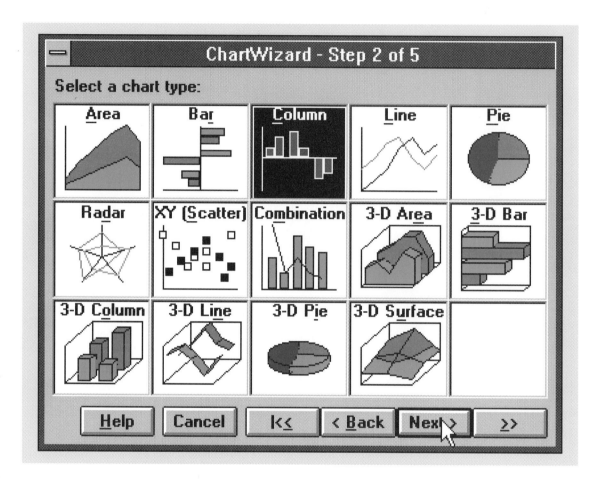

5. In the Step 2 dialog box, select Next.

The Step 3 dialog box will appear, showing format options for Column charts. In this case, you need to reset the option.

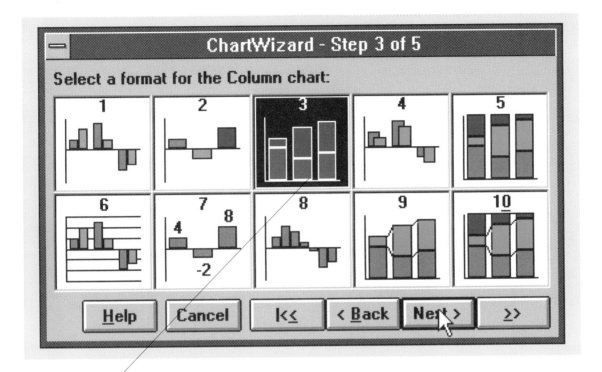

Changed from the default setting

6. In the Step 3 dialog box, click icon **3** (Stacked Columns).

7. Select **Next**.

The Step 4 dialog box will appear, containing a preview of the chart so far, along with some other option settings. You'll need to change some of these to make a more meaningful chart.

Quick Easy

8. In the Step 4 dialog box, select the **Columns** option button.

As soon as you select the option, the preview of the chart changes to show the result. This is the chart you want.

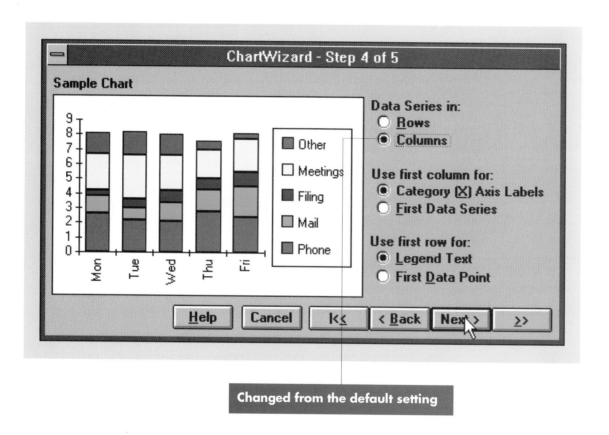

Changed from the default setting

9. Select **Next**.

The Step 5 dialog box will appear, in which you can enter titles for the chart and its axes. (You will leave the Add A Legend? option set to Yes.)

10. Click in the Chart Title text box and type **Productivity Study**. (Do *not* press ↵.)

11. Press **Tab** *twice* to advance to the Value box (skipping the Category box).

12. Type **Hours per Task**.

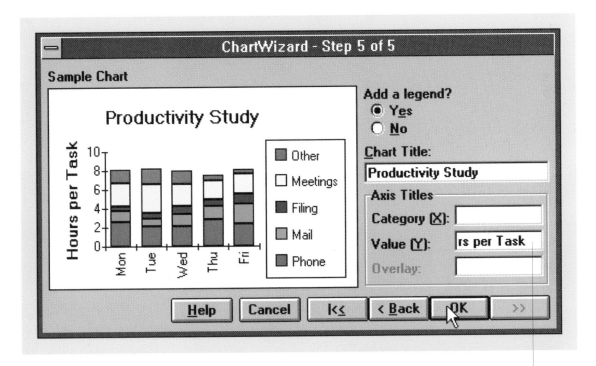

The entry is longer than the box, and the display scrolls.

13. Select **OK** to close the Step 5 dialog box.

Quick Easy

The completed chart will appear in the sheet, surrounded by handles, indicating that the chart as a whole is currently selected for further manipulation.

14. Adjust the vertical scroll bar so that the whole chart can be seen in the document window.

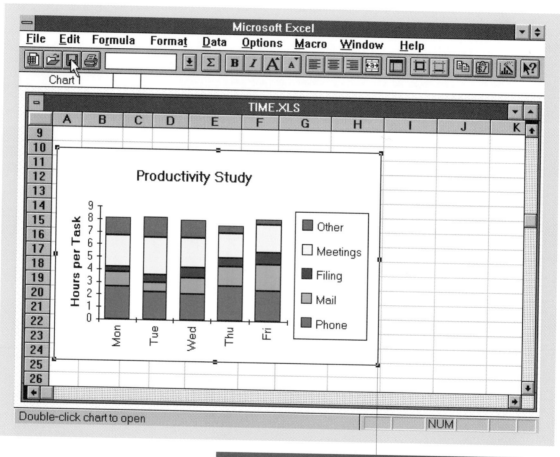

Handles show that the entire chart is selected.

15. Click the **Save File** tool to update the file TIME.XLS to include the chart.

In just a few steps, you have generated a chart that is both attractive and meaningful. You can now see at a glance just where your valuable time is going!

● Note You can preview or print this chart just as you would any sheet. Select File ➤ Print Preview or File ➤ Print.

Editing a Chart

Excel for Windows contains an extensive set of tools for manipulating charts of many different types. Now that you have built a chart and saved it to disk, try experimenting with just a few of these features.

Adding Grid Lines

You can add grid lines and edit other chart features by activating the Chart toolbar.

1. With the productivity chart still selected, move the pointer up to the toolbar and click the right mouse button. A shortcut menu will appear.

2. From the shortcut menu, select **Chart**. The Chart toolbar will appear.

3. Click the **Horizontal Gridlines** tool. Grid lines will appear in your chart.

Horizontal grid lines

Area Chart tool

Legend tool

Horizontal Gridlines tool

Notice the tool just to the right of the Gridlines tool. This is the Legend tool. It is already activated (and is shown as a depressed button) because you accepted the default legend setting previously. Clicking the Legend tool simply turns the legend display on or off, readjusting the chart composition each time.

Changing the Chart Type

It might be more dramatic to display the data in a different type of chart. You can do this literally at the click of a tool.

1. In the Chart toolbar, click the **Area Chart** tool. The stacked columns will change to layered areas.

2. Click the Control box (top-left corner) of the toolbar to make it disappear.

3. Click outside the chart area to release the selection.

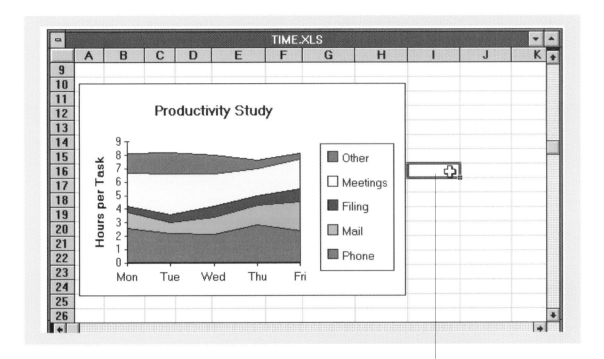

Click outside the chart to release it.

● **Note** The new chart is a different view of the same data. In this case, the areas are just as effective as the stacked columns in showing the relationships. However, depending on the information you are trying to present, some of the available chart types might not be appropriate or meaningful.

Quick Easy

Checking Your Spelling

One of the last things you might want to do after you have built a new sheet is to check the spelling of its text labels. Excel for Windows includes a built-in spelling checker that works the same as similar programs included with word processing software.

Quickly demonstrate this feature to yourself so that you can use it each time you finish a new sheet. In this example, you will also learn how you can edit objects in a chart.

1. Double-click on the productivity chart. The chart will re-appear in its own document window.

2. Double-click on the chart title. Hollow handles will appear around it, and its text will appear in the formula bar.

3. Type **Productivity Studyy**, adding the extra *y* as an intentional misspelling.

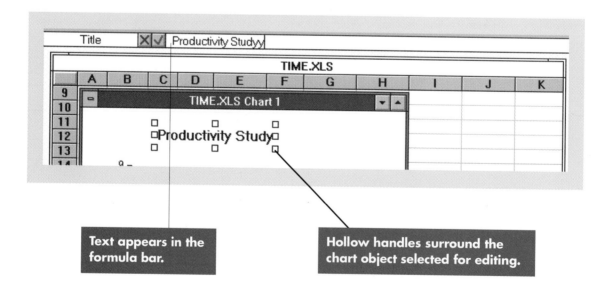

Text appears in the
formula bar.

Hollow handles surround the
chart object selected for editing.

4. Press ↵.

> **● Note** Whenever a chart is shown in its own document window, you can select objects within it for editing simply by clicking them. The selection is indicated by a set of hollow handles. For example, you could click a chart area and change its color by selecting Format ➤ Patterns.

5. Move the pointer to the toolbar and click the right mouse button. A shortcut menu will appear.

6. From the shortcut menu, select **Utility**. The Utility toolbar will appear.

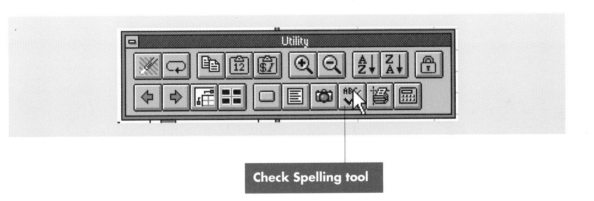

Check Spelling tool

7. In the Utility toolbar, click the **Check Spelling** tool (the icon labeled ABC ✓). The Spelling dialog box will appear.

Quick&Easy

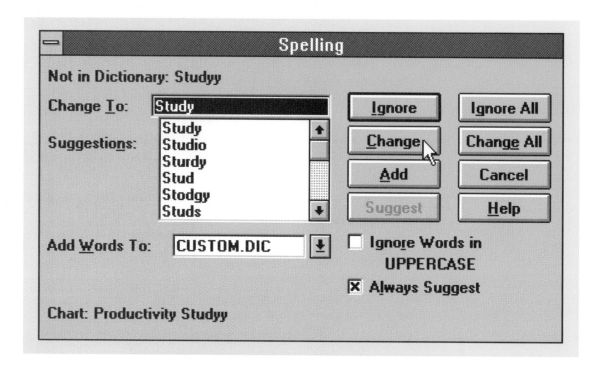

Words that Excel detects as possible misspellings will appear in the dialog box as Not In Dictionary. The closest match from the dictionary will appear in the Change To text box. Other possible selections will appear in the Suggestions list.

8. To accept the suggested spelling, select the **Change** button.

9. The program notifies you: "Finished spell checking current chart." Select **OK**.

> **● Note** If the correct spelling does not appear in the dialog box, type it in the Change To text box and then select Change.

Before you end this lesson, there is just one more thing you must do. (Hint: It involves the third tool from the left.)

Congratulations!

You have successfully completed ten brief but comprehensive lessons on designing worksheets to solve real-world business problems. You have learned all the basic skills you need to be productive with Excel for Windows, as well as some enhanced features that can make using the program even more quick and easy!

The most difficult part—learning a new program from scratch—is behind you. As you begin to build your own worksheets, there will be opportunities to extend your proficiency. Remember that all of the features of Excel 4—indeed, of all Windows applications—use the same, consistent set of controls and actions. Now that you are comfortable with these techniques, you will be able to learn new capabilities of Excel for Windows almost as soon as you discover them.

Appendix: Where Do I Go from Here?

In the short amount of time it's taken you to read this book, you've learned most of the things you'll ever need to know about Excel for Windows. Even the most advanced users of the program spend most of their time doing the things you've learned from this book. Still, you might reach a point where you want to know a little more about Excel's other capabilities. For example, you might want to learn how to use the program's Crosstab ReportWizard feature for cross-tabulation and what-if analysis, how to write powerful formulas that describe complex calculations, how to exchange data with external files and databases, or how to use advanced design features to create more attractive reports.

If you'd like to stick with a beginner's approach, learning in short, easy lessons and trying things out step-by-step, then **The ABC's of Excel 4 for Windows**, Alan R. Neibauer, SYBEX, 1992, is the right book for you. It covers the material in this book with a little more explanation, and then continues and explains some of the more useful advanced features.

If you think you're ready for a how-to book that doubles as a reference and covers Excel in depth, try **Mastering Excel 4 for Windows**, 2d ed., Carl Townsend, SYBEX, 1992. It's full of great examples and hands-on steps, and it explains everything from the most basic topics to the most advanced.

If you'd like a quick reference book to answer occasional questions, then you want **Excel 4 for Windows Instant Reference**, Douglas Hergert, SYBEX, 1992.

INDEX

●

A

account numbers, 118–119

active cells, 5

active windows, 144

addresses of cells, 5, 35–36, 147

aligning text, 20–21, 52, 54, 156

Alt-F4 key combination, 71

annotations, 137–141

apostrophe, 20

Area Chart tool, 170

Arrange Windows dialog box, 143–144

ascending sorts, 123

AutoFill tool, 35–37, 68, 156–159

AutoFormat tool, 74–77, 160

AutoSelect feature, 51

AutoSum tool, 10–11, 66–68, 124, 132

B

balances for check register, 29–39

blocks. *See* ranges

bold font, 78, 82, 85

BOOK1.XLW file, 152

Border dialog box, 84

borders, 82–85, 126–127

C

Cancel button, 7

caret (^), 20

Cell Note dialog box, 139–140

cell pointer, 5

cells, 4

  borders for, 82–85

  copying contents of, 33–35

  copying formats of, 80–81